Twayne's United States Authors Series

Sylvia E. Bowman, *Editor*
INDIANA UNIVERSITY

Marjorie Kinnan Rawlings

Courtesy of Charles Scribner's Sons

MARJORIE KINNAN RAWLINGS

MARJORIE KINNAN RAWLINGS

By SAMUEL I. BELLMAN

California State Polytechnic University, Pomona

 **241**

Twayne Publishers, Inc.   ::   New York

Library of Congress Cataloging in Publication Data
Bellman, Samuel Irving, 1926–
  Marjorie Kinnan Rawlings.

  (Twayne's United States authors series, TUSAS 241)
  Bibliography: p. 155.
  1. Rawlings, Marjorie (Kinnan) 1896–1953.
PS3535.A845Z57   813'.5'2   73–17291
ISBN 0–8057–0610–0

For Jeanne, Joel Ethan, and Jonathan David

Preface

My aim in writing this book about Marjorie Kinnan Rawlings has been to acquaint as many readers as possible with her work. Known widely for her Pulitzer Prize novel of 1938, *The Yearling*, she has the reputation of being a *mere* children's writer; and, partly because of this concept, she is generally ignored by the critics and by the official arbiters of literary fashion. Despite the initial success of her autobiographical *Cross Creek* (1940)— a Florida *Walden*—the book is seldom mentioned today; the fact that it is still kept in print in the Scribner Library paperback series does not change its status as a living fossil. A modest number of women here and there remember and cherish her Florida cookbook, *Cross Creek Cookery* (1942); but, however fascinating the personal remarks she has enlivened the book with, it too has done little to enhance her literary reputation. And her most suggestive stories are relatively unknown today—"Jacob's Ladder," "Gal Young Un," "A Mother in Mannville," "Cocks Must Crow"—although one of these may on occasion be reprinted. For example, "A Mother in Mannville" was reprinted in *Parents Magazine & Better Homemaking* in 1965 and in *Reader's Digest* in 1968. It is trite to resort to a pedantic plea that renewed attention must be given at last to an unjustly neglected writer, but the fact remains that Mrs. Rawlings' colorful fictions of rural Florida life and of man versus his environment entitle her to a new hearing (and reading) today.

In order to present a meaningful picture of Mrs. Rawlings the writer, I have chosen to include, in my first chapter, a series of "partial portraits"—glimpses, impressions, recollections, evaluations—from a wide variety of sources. Among these are people who had been close to her as well as people who had known her slightly or not at all; and there are also a few candid, revealing statements by Mrs. Rawlings herself. It is impossible for a reader to form any kind of opinion about her contribution to American letters unless he has some idea of her distinguishing characteristics, her background, her life-course.

Following this montage of "partial portraits" I examine in some detail each of her major works: her first three novels—*South Moon Under, Golden Apples, The Yearling*; her short story collection, *When the Whippoorwill*; her autobiographical *Cross Creek* and its companion volume, *Cross Creek Cookery*; and, finally, her last novel, *The Sojourner*.

The Yearling, I feel, is by far the most important of all of these works; accordingly, I devote considerably more space to it than to any of the other books. Much of what Mrs. Rawlings wrote throughout her life anticipates or reflects the central concern in *The Yearling*: the joys and sorrows of a young boy, and his relationship with his parents. One of the major influences in her life and thought was an image, an ideal, of a little boy of her own, the son she was unfortunately destined never to have. So that the discussion of that unusually fine book might be more informative, I have chosen to illuminate *The Yearling* against the background of Mrs. Rawlings' juvenilia, some of her early journalistic efforts, and a number of her shorter fictions. These "background" writings, taken together, reveal what her young hero in *The Yearling*, Jody Baxter, really meant to her; and they also help to explain how she was able in this work, if in no other, to articulate an almost universal longing into an enduring saga of a child entering upon manhood. In conclusion I briefly summarize Mrs. Rawlings' literary career and offer a few comments about her contributions to twentieth-century American literature.

Unfortunately, very little has been written about Mrs. Rawlings besides brief book notices and journalistic comment, human interest sketches of the "A Visit With . . ." variety, several obscure academic theses and literary introductions, and a single brief literary biography, Gordon E. Bigelow's *Frontier Eden*.

Professor Bigelow, a member of the English Department at the University of Florida, Gainesville, has drawn on the abundant resources of the Rawlings collection housed there for his human-interest account of her career as a writer. Making use of his own long familiarity with the North Florida region, he has stressed in his study the Florida setting that informed much of her best writing and that harmonized so well with her own introverted personality.

Preface

Since it was not Bigelow's intention to analyze systematically her most substantial work, the present volume in the Twayne Series, while making some use of his valuable book, is not to be taken as an attempt to furrow a plowed field. My aim, as already indicated, is to make Mrs. Rawlings' writings known to today's readers. Hopefully, this study will provide a basis for understanding Mrs. Rawlings as a writer among other American writers and as a sensitive woman who stamped her personality upon what she wrote.

A major source of inspiration in the preparation of this book was my visit, in the summer of 1966, with Mrs. Rawlings' three paternal aunts, the Misses Grace, Wilmer, and Marjorie Kinnan, in Phoenix, Arizona. Miss Grace Kinnan, who acted as spokeswoman for the family, very graciously placed at my disposal a sizable body of memorabilia: letters, newspaper clippings, magazines—a wealth of important documents relating to Mrs. Rawlings' life and work. Thus I came to know the famous author in a way that would otherwise have been impossible.

As I discussed Mrs. Rawlings with these three kind and charming ladies in their homes, I soon became aware of their deep, abiding love for her and of the pride they took in her accomplishments. Ever since that visit I have felt a kind of special attachment to the subject of this volume, which the numerous delays in writing have intensified rather than abated. While my findings and conclusions remain a private matter, I have tried in these pages to bring out some of the essential Majorie Kinnan Rawlings that is generally unknown to the reading public.

I wish to express my gratitude to the administration of California State Polytechnic University, Pomona, for a one-quarter Creative Leave in the winter of 1969 so that I could continue working on this book. And, I wish to thank the following:

(1) Mrs. Rawlings' publisher, Charles Scribner's Sons, for permission to quote from her books;

(2) The University of Florida Press (Gainesville) for permission to quote from Gordon E. Bigelow, *Frontier Eden: The Literary Career of Marjorie Kinnan Rawlings*, Copyright © 1966 by the Board of Commissioners of State Institutions of Florida;

(3) The National Audubon Society for material reprinted from

Audubon, the magazine of the National Audubon Society; Copyright © 1970;

(4) David McKay Company, Inc., for permission to quote from M. Esther Harding, *Journey Into Self,* Copyright © 1956.

Mr. Charles Scribner of Scribner's has been particularly generous in allowing me to quote extensively from Mrs. Rawlings' books.

Finally, I extend warm thanks to the many people who wrote to me about Mrs. Rawlings in response to a query of mine in the *New York Times* some years ago. While I was not able to use all of the material they so kindly provided me, I have incorporated a certain amount, indicating individual sources in my notes.

—SAMUEL IRVING BELLMAN

California State Polytechnic University, Pomona
Pomona, California

Contents

Contents

Chronology

1896 Marjorie Kinnan Rawlings born August 8 in Washington, D.C., to Arthur Frank Kinnan and Ida May Traphagen Kinnan.

1900 Brother, Arthur Houston Kinnan, born.

1907 Earned first money from writing ($2.00), for a story entered in a prize contest in the *Washington* (D.C.) *Post*. Had been "writing" since the age of six.

1912 Won second prize in the *McCall's* "Child Authorship Contest" with story "The Reincarnation of Miss Hetty," which appeared in the August issue of *McCall's*.

1913 Father, with whom she had been very close, died on January 31.

1914 After high-school graduation, moved with mother and brother to Madison, Wisconsin. Entered University of Wisconsin.

1914– At University of Wisconsin, became a prominent member
1918   of "Red Domino," the campus dramatic society. Wrote a fantasy, "Into the Nowhere," for "Union Vodvil." Acted in campus production of *A Midsummer Night's Dream*. Member of Delta Gamma (sorority) and Mortar Board (women's honor society). Made Phi Beta Kappa in junior year. Graduated with Bachelor of Arts degree.

1918– Worked as a publicist for the Young Women's Christian
1919   Association at National Headquarters in New York City.

1919 Married writer and boating enthusiast Charles A. Rawlings. Took up residence in Rochester, New York.

1919– Did advertising and newspaper writing: *Louisville Courier-*
1928   *Journal*; *Rochester Journal*; United Features Syndicate. Tried to publish her fiction.

1928 Bought a seventy-two-acre orange grove (four thousand trees) at Cross Creek, Hawthorne, Florida.

1930   First success with fiction: "Cracker Chidlings" (a series of sketches) bought by *Scribner's Magazine*. Second story, "Jacob's Ladder," also bought by *Scribner's*. Scribner's editor Maxwell Perkins began working with her.

1931   "Jacob's Ladder," published in the April issue of *Scribner's*, won second prize in the 1931 Scribner Prize Contest. Went to live for several weeks in the Big Scrub country (not far from Cross Creek) with the Fiddia family, an old woman and her moonshiner son.

1933   Divorced Charles Rawlings; continued to live at Cross Creek. Story "Gal Young Un" (originally published in the June, 1932, issue of *Harper's*), won first prize in the O. Henry Memorial Award contest for short stories. First novel published: *South Moon Under*, a Book-of-the-Month Club selection. Lived for a time with another family in the Big Scrub; gathered story material; made a brief trip to England for same reason.

1934   Made boat trip to Alaska with her brother Arthur and his wife Winifred.

1935   Second novel published: *Golden Apples*. Broke her neck in a fall from her horse.

1936   Sojourned in the mountains at Banner Elk, North Carolina. Met a little orphan boy there; he inspired her to write two stories about an orphan and a lady who wanted to be his mother: "A Mother in Mannville" (1936) and *Mountain Prelude* (1947).

1938   Third novel published: *The Yearling*, which was remarkably successful—Book-of-the-Month Club selection, movie rights sold to Metro-Goldwyn-Mayer.

1939   Awarded membership in National Institute of Arts and Letters. Won Pulitzer Prize in fiction for *The Yearling*. Granted the degree of Doctor of Letters by Rollins College. Taught a course in creative writing at the University of Florida, Gainesville. Spoke on "Regional Literature of the South" at the annual meeting of the National Council of Teachers of English.

1940   Published a short story collection: *When the Whippoorwill*.

1941   Awarded the degree of Doctor of Humane Letters by the

University of Florida. Married Norton Sanford Baskin. Established residence in St. Augustine, Florida.

1942 Published her autobiography: *Cross Creek* (Book-of-the-Month Club selection). Awarded degree of Doctor of Literature by the University of Tampa (Florida). Published *Cross Creek Cookery*.

1943 Libel suit entered against her by Zelma Cason. Case continued for next several years.

1945 Won O. Henry Memorial Award for story "Black Secret" (*The New Yorker*, September 8, 1945).

1946 Trial of libel case held in Gainesville. Decision for defendant; plaintiff appealed and case brought (for the second time) before State Supreme Court. Metro-Goldwyn-Mayer movie of *The Yearling* finally appeared (earlier version had been abandoned some years before).

1947 Florida Supreme Court decided against Mrs. Rawlings in libel suit; she was directed to pay Zelma Cason nominal damages. Novelette *Mountain Prelude* published in *The Saturday Evening Post*. Spent summer in Van Hornesville, New York, where she bought an old farmhouse that was to become her summer home.

1953 Last novel published: *The Sojourner*, a Literary Guild selection. Began working on a biography of Ellen Glasgow. Died on December 14, in St. Augustine, of a cerebral hemorrhage. Buried in a cemetery in Island Grove, Florida.

1955 Posthumous publication of children's book, *The Secret River*.

CHAPTER 1

Partial Portraits of a Lady

I *Marjorie Kinnan Rawlings*

Abhorring cities, she took her secret hurt
Into the flat-woods: another De León
In search of healing waters.
The marriage failed but Florida
Was balm, and out poured tales
Of Cracker ways, a whole
New language for the proud
Tormented soul. Her cooking
Graced her life, a fierce disjointed
Thing, compact of solitude and
Work at orange grove and desk.
Her legacies were rich but somehow often sad:
The way it used to be, in hammock land and scrub,
The code for tasty meals,
Some pictures of the boy she never had.
Her biggest foe was Time,
But when she'd learnt enough to
Go and make her peace,
It turned and claimed her.
She never knew
The soft and slow release.[1]

How best to convey the biting flavor of Mrs. Rawlings' bitter-sweet sojourn on earth? Not by a detailing of landmark dates or a dutiful recitation of her comings and goings. What *is* an author's life, to a preoccupied outsider? There is an inscription on Mrs. Rawlings' tombstone: "By her writing, she endeared herself to the people of the world." [2] Her life was in what she had written for others to read, but this contribution cannot be fairly summarized. Her life was in the series of impressions she had left on everyone around her, but those were too long ago and too

[17]

far away to be correctly captured. And yet her life remains, in a series of partial portraits, drawn by divers hands.

From a newspaper feature story in 1942, this thumbnail sketch emerges. Mrs. Rawlings' paternal grandmother wrote verse. Her father's family included several Methodist ministers, one of whom published a philosophical work. Her American heritage could be traced back to the time of the American Revolution. On both sides of the family her ancestors were Scotch and Scotch-Irish, and Holland Dutch. When she was a young girl, her parents encouraged her to use the family library. A studious child, she soon made favorites of Sir Walter Scott and Charles Dickens. Her literary interests continued over the years; when she attended the University of Wisconsin, she majored in English. She was also a member of the Dramatics Club and Kappa Alpha Theta, and was elected to Phi Beta Kappa. She contributed to all the school publications, serving on the editorial staff of the literary magazine and the year book.

While an undergraduate she composed a pantomime fantasy called "Into the Nowhere." Copyrighted by the Dramatics Club, it was popular with her classmates; for a number of years it was performed by drama groups in colleges and schools across the country. Fredric March was one of her classmates; both used to appear in the same amateur productions of the Dramatics Club. After graduation, she entered the field of journalism and started with news writing. She and her editor at the *Rochester* (New York) *Journal* would go through the day's news stories for human interest leads, and she would then write the features. Her news-writing experience was enjoyable. She felt that news writing served as an excellent preparation for would-be writers. In her view, it taught objectivity; and the logical next step was good imaginative writing.[3]

A fellow alumna from the University of Wisconsin, Mrs. Dorothy S. Helmer, had the following to say of her in a letter to this writer from Encinitas, California, June 22, 1965:

In my college snapshot album I have a page size picture of the cast of "Into the Nowhere"—a Columbine-Harlequin-Pierette-Pierrot sort of fantasy written by Marjorie Kinnan for Union Vodvil. Marjorie is in the foreground (Columbine). . . . I have a larger picture of her in costume in a production of 'Midsummer Night's Dream.' . . . Later on

Marjorie wrote of herself as *plain*. Maybe that was after Dora (?) her jersey cow added on the pounds. But I do not remember her as at all *plain*. She was a tall, small-boned, small-featured slip of a girl, reed slender, willowy and graceful with black hair, clear, high color and Irish blue eyes. Rather an angular, slightly lop-sided little face, pixyish, and very pretty withal. She was a dancer, some ballet I think and 'aesthetic dancing' as we used to call it,—sort of free form with floating draperies and long scarves. When she wrote of dancing in the moonlight in her Florida orchard I could well imagine her there!

Another fellow student, who had worked with her on the *Lit* magazine, commented in a newspaper book review of *South Moon Under* in 1933: " 'She wrote verses . . . about "Little Grey Town of Tumbledown" and other places hard to locate geographically because they existed only in her lively fancy. About real places or real people she did not write, having had little experience of them, and withdrawing, in fact, from hateful contacts with reality which might cloud the bright world of imagination where she felt more at home.' " [4] Recently, yet another Wisconsin graduate recalled, in a letter to the present writer, those memorable college days. Marjorie Kinnan, whom she came to know well, "was a charming and attractive person, with great warmth and insight."

She was a fellow sorority sister of mine in Kappa Kappa Gamma at the University of Wisconsin. When I was a sophomore and she was perhaps a senior we both instigated, worked for and recruited a group of sorority girls whose aim was to abolish the system. Somewhere in my records I have our printed manifesto, in pamphlet form, to the effect that snobbish Greek letter societies had no place in state universities. We waxed eloquent and managed to gain publicity in the news services and I believe either the *Nation* or *New Republic*. In those days—perhaps now—Jews were excluded from these sororities. Nobody even thought to mention Negroes; so far as I know none even applied for membership. At Kappa Kappa Gamma during one pledging there was great soul searching about accepting Pauline Pabst, because of her beer connection, but we finally took her because of her comfortable situation, thanks to the beer connection.

We had eighteen or twenty of the girls from the major sororities. President Van Hise's daughter, Alice, Professor Richard T. Ely's daughter, most of the gifted and talented girls, and Marjorie went right up to the final ultimatum. On a given night each of us rose in holy meeting and turned in her pin. We felt that the final blow had been struck and were amazed at what a small dent we made. At the very end Marjory got cold feet—she still believed heartily in all we stood for and had worked for faithfully, but her beau—as we called them then— Chuck Rawlings, finally convinced her not to blight herself socially by really resigning. I remember tears and great emotion before she finally [left us].

Even in those days her writing promise showed brilliantly. Professor R. E. N. Dodge, a brilliant English professor, who had us prospective writers turning in a daily story, predicted rightly that she would be a most significant addition to American letters.[5]

In 1919, she married Charles Rawlings, by now a newspaper-man deeply attached to the sea (later his yachting stories appeared frequently in *The Saturday Evening Post*). Two journalists and would-be fiction writers in a family of two? What of the woman's traditional role of homemaker? In a newspaper interview in 1926, Mrs. Rawlings made some interesting remarks about her position. She had been brought up to believe in the modern myth that housekeeping is only drudgery, and the housewife a downtrodden martyr. Thus, when beginning to take care of her own home, she felt that she had joined the ranks of the mistreated. After a time came the realization that she didn't feel at all downtrodden; she was, in fact, thoroughly enjoying herself. For her there was romance in housework, as well as charm and whimsy and humor without end. (But application and effort are required.) " 'I have found,' " the journalist-homemaker said, " 'that the housewife works hard, of course—but likes it. Most people who amount to anything do work hard, at whatever their job happens to be.' " [6]

For years, she had tried serious writing, and gained only a rich collection of rejection slips. Would her move to Cross Creek in the Florida back country, in 1928, change matters? For a time, conditions remained as discouraging as they had been before; then, in March, 1930, just when she was about to abandon all hope of becoming a writer, the wheel of fortune turned. An important literary monthly, *Scribner's*, accepted her "Cracker Chidlings," a series of sketches of Cracker life. Later that year *Scribner's* accepted her story "Jacob's Ladder." However, the publication of her first efforts brought some unfavorable reaction from the Cross Creek area; some Floridians said that there were

"no such people" as the ones she wrote about, but such was not
the case. The mother of one of the characters that she used
spotted him in the story and threatened to whip the author to
death.[7]

The incompatibility of a *writing* husband and wife, when they
are not really a team, had been felt by the couple for some time
before the move to Florida. And the new locale, as it turned out,
did not really bring them closer together:

. . . in spite of an occasional lift, as when they saved the bean crop
from frost to make a spectacular profit, Charles had become increasingly bored with the routine of Cross Creek life. . . . About a month
after the book [*South Moon Under*] was published [1933], Perkins
[her editor at Scribner's] sent [her] a big manila envelope full of
reviews clipped from all over the United States and England. Nearly
all were full of praise for the new talent. Here was the fame for which
she had yearned so long, but instead of filling her with elation, it sent
her into a mood of intense melancholy. . . . She looked up from the
reviews with such misery that Charles asked her if she wanted to be
alone. She said yes. He packed and left for the seacoast, and they both
understood that he was not coming back.[8]

In 1936, she met Ernest Hemingway in the Bahamas, and she
wrote Maxwell Perkins (who was also Hemingway's editor at
Scribner's) her impressions of the belligerent bruiser who appeared so gentle and sensitive (and who told her he greatly
admired her writing). " 'There is, obviously, some inner conflict in
Hemingway which makes him go about his work with a chip
on his shoulder, and which makes him want to knock people
down. He is so great an artist that he does not need to be ever on
the defensive. He is so vast, so virile, that he does not need ever
to hit anybody. Yet he is constantly defending something that he,
at least, must consider vulnerable.' " A conflict in him between the
sporting life and the literary life? Hemingway, she observed,
spent a great deal of time among sporting people, who responded
to him strongly. She surmised that he unconsciously valued what
they thought and feared to reveal to them " 'the agony that tears
the artist. He must be afraid of lifting before them the curtain
that veils the beauty that should be exposed only to reverent
eyes.' "[9]

That same year, while staying for a time in the Carolina

mountains, she met another Scribner's "great," F. Scott Fitzgerald, who was recuperating in Asheville from various disorders (his autobiographical revelation, "The Crack-Up," had recently appeared in *Esquire*). The impression he made on her was that " 'of the true artist, who had been conditioned to false values, and that while he understood that the values were spurious, could not disassociate himself from them. . . . I know just what his state of mind has been. The same kind of panic hits anyone like me, with no one dependent on me.' " What with his family difficulties, and other problems—" ' "the times," as Hemingway wrote me, "when you can't do it"—it was natural enough for him to go into a very black mood. It lasted longer and he publicized it more than most of us—I am always ashamed to let anyone know about mine . . .' " [10]

Moving to the North Florida backwoods had helped make her what she probably would never have been otherwise, a successful writer. She was to become closely identified with this particular region of Florida, and her very best writing was to be seen as a reflection of the region. But she could state, in a public address in 1939, that " 'I don't hold any brief for regionalism, and I don't hold with the regional novel as such. If people really are just as quaint as all-get-out, write an essay about them for the National Geographic, but don't make a novel about them unless they have a larger meaning than just quaintness.' " [11]

A lively, alert woman full of strongly held ideas, Mrs. Rawlings revealed in her newspaper interviews (particularly after she had gained a large measure of fame) how hard it would be for age to stale her, or custom wither. There was, for example, an interview with a reporter for the *Christian Science Monitor* in the fall of 1940 who asked her if she would write a sequel to *The Yearling*. She replied that she would not; the book was complete. What would Jody Baxter, the novel's young hero, have been like when he was grown? " 'Like Penny [Jody's father], who is my favorite character. Penny expresses my own philosophy—that life knocks a person down; and he gets up, and it knocks him down again. And that the only strong, manly thing for a man to do when he's down is to take the experience calmly and go on—that is, get up and go at it again.' " Did she have a hobby? Yes, cooking was her hobby, her one vanity: " 'I get as much satisfaction from preparing a perfect dinner for a few good friends as from turning turning out a perfect paragraph in my writing.' " [12]

Mrs. Rawlings accepted the natural environment the way she took people: on her own terms. An unusually complex person, even for a dedicated writer, either she was at war with herself much of the time or she harbored at least two distinct person- alities. For example, there is the matter of the outdoor life, in regard to which she projected a striking picture of the dedicated sportswoman. Yet a close observer pointed out in 1943 that "she is a very poor shot. And when she hunts, her aim is so poor her friends have caught on. She doesn't want to hit anything. She loves to tramp the woods with her bird dogs, watch them work a field, and point a covey of quail. Then Marjorie kicks the birds up and watches them buzz away." [13]

Her second marriage, in 1941, was far more successful than her first. References in *Cross Creek* (1942) make it clear that her new husband, Norton Sanford Baskin, was an old friend for whom she had a great deal of respect. Mr. Baskin was a restaura- teur and hotel operator, and at the time of their marriage he was managing the Castle Warden Hotel in St. Augustine. Although she was now obliged to move to St. Augustine to be with him, there is little indication that she gave up her solitary pursuits or became much more social than she had been earlier. A reporter illustrated their "private lives" approach with the following anecdote: "An interior decorator from New York was visiting in St. Augustine. She had heard about Castle Warden and paid the hotel a visit. Mr. Baskin was conducting her through one of the suites when the woman exclaimed, 'How lovely! I see the fine hand of Marjorie Kinnan Rawlings in this place.' To which Norton replied politely, 'No, Madam. You do *not* see Mrs. Rawlings' fine hand in this place. Nor will you see my big foot in her next book. That's our agreement. She writes. I run a hotel.'" [14]

The war years brought Mrs. Rawlings (she was still referred to by this name) new problems and hardships. Her husband became an ambulance driver for the American Field Service, and spent over a year at great personal risk aiding the war effort in the Far East. Difficult as his absence and a protracted illness following his tour of duty in Asia were for her, there was also a long-drawn-out libel suit brought against her by a former Cross Creek friend, Zelma Cason. According to her biographer, Gordon Bigelow:

Her misjudgment of Zelma Cason was to cost her a painful and expensive legal process which dragged on for more than five years. . . . Zelma Cason was one of [her] oldest Florida friends. . . . This "friendship" was only one complicating factor in an unusually complex legal action, which began on January 8, 1943, when Zelma entered suit against [her] for libel, asking $100,000 damages. The nature of the suit was so ambiguous that it required eighteen months of legal maneuvering, including a decision of the Florida Supreme Court, to determine if adequate grounds for legal action existed. The state Supreme Court ruled that grounds existed if the charge was changed from libel to "invasion of privacy," and then nearly two years elapsed before the case was brought to trial in May of 1946. . . . Zelma's case was based upon the claim that several passages in *Cross Creek* had caused her great pain and humiliation, chiefly one passage from pages 48–49. . . . When the verdict was announced there was an ovation from the audience, which had been overwhelmingly favorable to [Marjorie's] cause throughout.[15]

In a letter to her aunts in Phoenix, Mrs. Rawlings discussed her winning of the case. Fifty-one witnesses had testified on her behalf, either out of love or out of plain honesty. "It has all proved what I have been writing about for many years," she commented, "that these plain country folk are *good* and friendly people." [16] But Mrs. Rawlings really lost, in the end. The plaintiff appealed, and, in the words of Mrs. Rawlings' biographer,

. . . for a second time the case went to the State Supreme Court, which a year later in a 3–4 decision rendered a compromise verdict, reversing the finding of the lower court but stipulating only token damages of one dollar. . . . In spite of the ultimate unfavorable decision of the Supreme Court, [she] felt one resounding victory in the whole unpleasant business, and that was the response of her neighbors and friends. . . . Nevertheless, the trial on the whole was a bitter experience which exacted a heavy cost, not only in money, but in worry and distraction and in energy she could little spare from her writing . . .[17]

For a number of reasons Mrs. Rawlings in her declining years turned farther and farther away from the place she had called home for so long. The environment was no longer "right" for her, and she felt the need for at least a summer home in the East—upstate New York, perhaps. In the light of what she was to write in her last novel, *The Sojourner* (1953), which is set, oddly enough, in that part of the country, the following remarks by an old friend of hers, an attorney in Cooperstown, New York, are significant. Mrs. Rawlings "had been coming to Van Hornesville in the County of Herkimer for several years and on January 10, 1947, she purchased a parcel of land containing approximately ten acres in the Town of Springfield, Otsego County, New York, on which there was a frame one and one-half story house which was architecturally very attractive and was many years old and in a run-down condition. [She] remodeled the interior of this house and made it very attractive . . . [and] occupied the above home for about six to eight months every year until her death."[18]

II *Release*

The rambling house, which looked out toward Otsego Lake, had actually been built in 1848, and the property on which the house was located was part of the original General Philip Schuyler grant. There was an Adams mantle in the living room; over the mantle hung a painting, which she had picked up at the Smithy, an antique shop in Cooperstown. But pleasant as the house was, it could not be the focus of her life; her winters were still spent in Florida so that she could be near her husband. Before leaving Springfield, New York, in the fall, she would first telephone Norton at Marineland to let him know when she would be coming home. During the winter, she stayed in her cottage near St. Augustine or in her old home in Cross Creek.[19] During one of these winter returns, after she had completed what must be called her valedictory novel, *The Sojourner*, death claimed her.

A friend, Mrs. Lillian May, described her last hours in a letter to her aunts in Phoenix. Mrs. Rawlings and her husband Norton had been staying at Crescent Beach. For some time she had been troubled with diverticulitis, and on Thursday evening, December 10 (1953), she complained of a pain in her stomach. She remained in bed until Monday morning, when Norton had her taken to the hospital in St. Augustine. There, the doctor said that he feared a small blood vessel at the base of the brain had broken. In the afternoon, another small blood vessel ruptured. That night she had another attack, and died. The postmortem examination revealed that death was due to cerebral hemorrhage. The little cemetery at Island Grove was chosen for her final resting place because, when she had attended the funeral of a friend there about two years before, she had remarked, " 'I could rest here.' " There were many cedar trees in the cemetery and several oaks. It was a quiet, restful spot with simple gravestones, as well as a clean, windswept aspect and many birds.[20]

Norton Baskin, in a letter to the aunts, described the funeral. After her death, there was a service in St. Augustine at the chapel of the funeral home. The Episcopal minister read the beautiful and simple ceremony. Before the service, Norton asked their long-time friend and lawyer, Philip May, to say a few words. Mr. May spoke very briefly and then read the last paragraph of *Cross Creek*, which begins: "Who owns Cross Creek? The red-birds, I think, more than I, for they will have their nests even in the face of delinquent mortgages. And after I am dead, who am childless, the human ownership of grove and field and hammock is hypothetical." After the services were concluded, her body was taken for burial to the Antioch Cemetery at Island Grove, four miles from Cross Creek. The minister read the interment service, and after that Mr. May spoke again and read the last paragraph of *Cross Creek*.[21]

In another letter to his wife's aunts, Norton Baskin described the disposition of Mrs. Rawlings' estate and then added this unusual personal reminiscence: "Did I ever tell you that Marjorie was the shyest person I have ever known. This was always strange to me as she could stand up to anybody in any department of endeavor but time after time when she was asked to go some place or to do something she would accept—'if I would go with her.' "[22]

CHAPTER 2

A Dark Lunar Idyll: *South Moon Under*

I *Who Belongs in the Scrub?*

MRS. RAWLINGS' first novel, *South Moon Under*, is set in the Big Scrub country (the Ocala Scrub), which is also the setting of *The Yearling*. Much of this wilderness (or semi-wilderness) area is encompassed within what is now known as the "Ocala National Forest, [which is] approximately twenty by forty miles in extent, bordered by the St. Johns River on the east and the Oklawaha on the west." [1] Like some ominous but irresistible region of Thomas Hardy's Wessex (Egdon Heath, for example), it assumes the status of a character in the story.

Probably the major reason for this "first" novel's effectiveness is Mrs. Rawlings' having prepared herself so well for its composition. By some happy inspiration, she arranged to spend several weeks, in the latter part of 1931, in the primeval scrub country, living with an old woman and her son, who made his living by moonshining. This illicit but common occupation in the North Florida backwoods was to exercise an enormous fascination on Mrs. Rawlings. Many of her Cracker stories devote a good deal of attention to the 'shiners and to the details of setting up and operating a moonshine still. More than that, the entire experience of "going primitive" in the company of that congenial pair seemed to be just what she had needed to prime her imagination for a full-bodied novel of life in the scrub. And, just as Mrs. Rawlings was to take the old lady Piety Fiddia and her son Leonard and transform them into Piety Jacklin and her son Lant, so she was finally able to draw on a rich source of Cracker lore—the moon and its phases—for the emblematic title of the novel and produce a work that would become a Book-of-the-Month Club selection as well as a finalist in the Pulitzer Prize competition.

One of the controlling ideas in the book has to do with

belonging, and to understand what Mrs. Rawlings meant we may as well begin with a Bible reference, Amos 6:1–"Woe to them that are at ease in Zion . . ." " 'I've been uneasy all my life,' " Penny Baxter says at the conclusion of *The Yearling* (426). Asahel Linden, the protagonist of *The Sojourner*, never knows what to really feel at home means, although he remains on the family farm for the better part of a century; through him, in fact, Mrs. Rawlings is able to generalize about the plight of homelessness that characterizes the human condition. Again and again we discover in Mrs. Rawlings' stories that her important characters do not really *belong*. Whatever their claim to a piece of land or to a position of some sort, whatever their feeling of being in harmony with nature or with things in general, these characters are often in error. They do not belong, their dream of safety (to use Auden's words) has to disappear. What gives *South Moon Under* its distinctive character, what shapes the entire story, is the basic insecurity of the central figure at the beginning of the book and the comparable insecurity of his grandson at the very end.

Young Lant Jacklin is actually a kind of replica of old man Lantry, although the vagary of circumstance produces this similarity. *South Moon Under* opens with Lantry moving his wife and five children about twenty-five miles away from their former home, across the Oklawaha River and into the scrub country. Mrs. Rawlings was completely at home as she described the setting: the swamp cypress and the equally lush growth–bay, ash, hickory, magnolia, sweet gum, live oak, holly–in the hammock adjoining. The scrub plateau's western edge rose high. With the river running between forty and fifty feet below, the bank facing the scrub came up sharply from the swamp. To this forbidding region Lantry had brought his family, and here he had cleared a narrow piece of the hammock land atop the bank. There was some compelling reason for his choice; above all he sought (as many other Rawlings characters would do) the security of genuine isolation. No one else lived within ten miles of the area, above or below, and he would be–in theory at least–kept safe by the river, on the one hand, and by the scrub, on the other.

The reader is intrigued by Lantry's odd manner–a pent-up fury of sorts suggesting a man of violence. Yet all who knew him could attest to his basic outward calm. But we soon learn a little bit more about him, enough to provoke our curiosity further. At a peaceful fence-raising party Lantry, his family, and his guests are intruded upon by some wild, drunken rascals. An effort is made to tolerate these obnoxious party-crashers. Now in an expansive mood, Lantry calls the figures for the square dance, and one of the figures is unfamiliar to his guests. The intruders are taken by surprise: where could he have picked up that strange dance figure, and where is he from, anyway? Lantry is challenged directly; when he indicates he does not wish to reply, he is taunted by the intruders. But he retains his calm and curtly tells his interrogator to mind his own business. Somehow trouble is avoided. The rude strangers finally leave and then Lantry's invited guests depart also.

Now, closed in behind his new gates, Lantry has some of the protection he has been seeking; but, in a brief domestic sequence, his wife is upset with him for dancing with one of the other women. He riles up in return and orders her into the house. Strangely enough, as Mrs. Rawlings describes it, his wife and children were just as alien to him as were the others—with one exception. His daughter Piety, his favorite child, would always be close to him, united to him by a special bond. Now, he tells little Piety, he thinks they will be safe.

Five years later, Lantry has done rather well, for all his basic ineptitude at farming; but it is no secret, so far as Piety is concerned, how close he had come to losing everything. At this point, the author's comment is particularly significant: "There was something about the most fertile field that was beyond control. A man could work himself to skin and bones, so that there was no flesh left on him to make sweat in the sun, and a crop would get away from him. There was something about all living that was uncertain" (36).

Does Lantry have some peculiar dark secret that would account for his alienation? Seven years after he has moved his family into the scrub, his wife dies. Left alone now with his beloved daughter Piety, he admits to her that he has not been able to find peace and comfort; the trouble is, he has a peculiar recurring dream. In this dream someone at the river takes him by surprise, but he manages to run through the clearing and into the scrub to safety. Lantry begins to sweat at the recollection of this nightmare. Then, prompted by Piety, he admits just what it is that he is afraid of: he once killed a federal agent, back where he came from. (North Carolina, from the evidence in the novel.) He was making his own whiskey, moonshine whiskey, and federal revenue agents caught up with him. Somehow he became overly provoked and killed one of the men. Then he headed south; but, since that time, he has not been able to rest. Does anyone around where they are now know about it?, Piety inquires. Not for sure, Lantry answers, but at times it seems to him that someone suspects. Has anyone ever taken out after him? Lantry's answer is ironic: if so, they still haven't caught up with him . . . but he will always be thinking about it. As it happens, no one ever does track Lantry down, and the strange, emotionally repressed man is able to die under peaceful circumstances if not in a peaceful state of mind.

His grandson Lant, toward the end of the novel, is placed in almost the same unenviable position. Lant's cousin Cleve, a worthless rascal who is married to a girl Lant has long admired, leads the Prohibition agents to Lant's moonshine still, which they destroy. Cleve now promises to continue to be a serious threat to Lant and to the other settlers, including Abner Lantry, his and Lant's uncle. Real trouble is brewing, for there is much talk of how desirable it would be if Cleve weren't around any more; but Lant resists the idea of taking any drastic measures. And then one day Lant, poking disconsolately through the woods, alone, finds that Cleve is shadowing him closely with a lifted gun barrel.

Now, at Lant's moment of crisis, Mrs. Rawlings picks up the old familiar theme of physical insecurity (with its implications of the desirability of belonging safely somewhere) and begins to wrap up the story of the Lantrys, grandfather and grandson: "All his life, he knew now, he had been afraid of something. He had drunk a fear in his mother's milk and in the buck Zeke Lantry had given him in a hollow gourd. He had sucked it from the air old man Lantry had puffed out from his dying lungs. A fear pulsed in his veins like poison." What was Lant afraid of? "A soundless tracking at his back and a white pasty moon [Cleve's face] above the sparkleberries— He was blind with fear. Danger was a remembered danger, remembered in his bones and in his blood" (326). Without realizing it, Lant brings up his rifle, and Cleve is shot dead.

Was there something peculiar about Lant's having been put in this terrible position whereby he suddenly felt he had to kill his cousin? Yes, Mrs. Rawlings suggests strongly: ascribe the situation to the forces of nature, which lie entirely beyond human control. Specifically, the cause goes back to the position of the moon at the time—south-moon-under—that is, the moon riding high on the other side of the earth, and powerful enough to affect some of the small woodland creatures.

Lant, on behalf of the author, speculates as to whether humans too are "moved against their will." It would seem so: "A man ordered his life, and then an obscurity of circumstance sent him down a road that was not of his own desire or choosing. Something beyond a man's immediate choice and will reached through the earth and stirred him." Lant does not know how this power could be escaped by anyone (so strong are the author's anxieties here): "Neither river nor swamp nor hammock nor impenetrable scrub could save a man from the ultimate interference. There was no safety. There was no retreat. Forces beyond his control, beyond his sight and hearing, took him in their vast senseless hands when they were ready. The whole earth must move as the sun and moon and an obscure law directed—even the earth, planet-ridden and tormented" (327).

No place, then, can offer permanent security, not even the scrub—and yet, and yet. Now Cleve's widow, Kezzy, knowing what Lant has done to her husband, yet having herself turned against him when he betrayed his own people, offers herself to Lant. She is quite willing for him to be her man now, and take care of her two children. The murder? She grieves for both him and Cleve, but more for him. He had to do it, she figures. And they can always go back to the scrub itself, which is close by; and Kezzy admires the scrub mightily. In the event that they had to seek shelter and security somewhere else, she wouldn't mind in the least going there to make a new home; in fact, she would probably welcome the opportunity. No one could get the better of her there, she hints, on a note of defiance.

Thus the novel ends, with Lant not really knowing whether he will somehow, someday, be apprehended. But he has a feeling that he will. And Kezzy shows her children a female squirrel frozen still in a tree, pretending not to be there—probably because she has baby squirrels waiting for her in the nest.

II *"The moon, sweet regent of the sky"*
(William Mickle, "Cumnor Hall")

As with one of Thomas Hardy's better novels, there is a great deal of rustic folklore in *South Moon Under*. For example, after old man Lantry dies and is laid to rest, a light rain falls in the night. The next morning Piety tells her son, " 'Hit's always so. You take notice, son, hit'll always rain after a buryin'. Hit's planned so o' purpose. The rain washes out the tracks o' the dead along with the tracks o' the livin'. Hit wouldn't do to have the earth all yopped up with the tracks o' the dead' " (82). It is interesting, however, that Mrs. Rawlings has filled this symbolically titled novel with so many lunar references: the voluminous lore of the moon's phases and their importance in human affairs—hunting, planting, and certain other vital matters. There is a tide in the affairs of her characters, and the moon is one of its chief regulators.

The time of the story is early in the twentieth century. When Lant Jacklin is fourteen, he is already in possession of a vast amount of Cracker nature lore. As wise in the ways of the great outdoors as he is ignorant of the world of books, he is quite able to hold his own with seasoned veterans of the woods, such as old man Paine. *Lant*: " 'Moon-rise 'bout a hour after sun tonight.' " *Paine*: " 'Finest kind o' time for the deer.' " *Lant*: " 'Moon-down's jest as good.' " When Piety objects to her son's acting so biggety, the old man defends him (as a fellow votary): " 'Why, the boy's right. . . . He knows the deer feeds on the moon, like most ary wild creeter. Four times the deer feeds. Stirs or feeds. Moon-rise and moon-down, and south-moon-over and south-moon-under. Come moon-rise, say, the deer's done been sleepin', ain't they? They comes out about a hour 'fore the moon. They feeds a while and frolics a while.' " Soon the old man adds a footnote: " 'Hit's jest my idee . . . favourin' moon-rise. Seem to me the deer's hongrier and more keerless' " (100–01).

Soon Lant is in the woods, alone. The moon is almost full. He sees it at its zenith and hears the cries of the hoot-owls. And he thinks that it must now be south-moon-over, and time for their feeding. Going home through the woods, Lant reflects on the moon and the deer, as well as on the owls and the fish. The animals "stirred at moon-rise and at moon-down; at south-moon-over and at south-moon-under. The moon swung around the earth, or the earth swung around the moon, he was not sure. The moon rose in the east and that was moon-rise. Six hours later it hung at its zenith between east and west, and that was south-moon-over. It set in the west and that was moon-down. Then it passed from sight and swung under the earth, between west and east. And when it was directly under the earth, that was south-moon-under." The moon's influence on the animals' living habits made sense to Lant, who was able to read all of the marks plainly. But it was still cause for amazement to him that, when the moon was all the way over on the earth's opposite side, it could affect the animals so strongly. Far, far distant, and unable to be seen by any of them, the moon continued to make its strength felt (109–10).

Sometime after this episode, Lant, now sixteen, is caught up in a little intimidation game whereby he helps frighten away an intruding settler (from Alabama, as it happens) who violates the custom of the country. On one occasion in the course of Lant's secret maneuverings against the outlander, Lant is able to tell that the south moon is under him—the night being dark—by the noises that the rabbits and hoot-owls make. On another occasion, Kezzy and Lant's mother are engaging in women talk. Kezzy asks Piety if she will be doing her butchering " 'on this moon.' " Piety answers, regretfully, that she and Lant won't be able to: the next week would be just right for them, but not right in terms of the moon, which at that time will be waning. Kezzy agrees that that is no time to do any butchering—the meat will only shrivel when it is being fried. This fact makes her ponder on the queerness of the moon's ways. Piety goes along with her as far as the shrinking of the meat is concerned, but disagrees that there is something queer about the way the moon affects crop growth: " 'Plantin' root crops, like onions and 'taters, when the nights is dark, makes sense. Plantin' top crops between new moon and full, that makes sense. The moon draws the leaves outen the ground, same as the sun.' " And Kezzy says: " 'Hit don't make sense makin' soap on the full moon nor pickin' sage leaves' " (188–89).

Lant, of course, knows how otters are affected by the lunar cycle—he points out that they slide on the moon's four quarters. Later, when he and his mother discuss hunting, she calls his attention to the moon and reminds him that he intended to get after the buck that will be back eating their sweet potatoes that night. He has been noticing the moon, he assures her, and then invites Kezzy to go with him about moon-down to kill the predator. They set out, and "a yellow half-moon [hangs] low between two palms" (212, 214).

Lant goes fishing; and, in describing the action, Mrs. Rawlings preserves the lunar rhythms of her story. He had aimed to make it to "the creek at south-moon-over, but the moon was an hour past the meridian when they began to work the lines. The catch was only four fish" (248). And there is even a passing reference to physical dependence on the moon—although the reference is bio-functional rather than folklorist. Thus, growing old, Piety develops cataracts on her eyes, and she tells Kezzy that she has become "'moon-eyed'": only when the moon is shining brightly can she see clearly (287). Near the end of the novel, Cleve's face (at the time he has alienated everyone by his treachery and Lant shoots him) is described as an evil moon. After the shooting, Lant hears hoot-owls; it is south-moon-under. Again Mrs. Rawlings refers to the moon's power to affect (from a great distance) the woodland creatures.

A passage in Thomas Hardy's *The Return of the Native* (1878) deals with moon-talk and lunar influences on birthlings. Christian Cantle, the village eunuch, had been born when there was no moon: "'Mother know'd 'twas no moon, for she asked another woman that had an almanac, as she did whenever a boy was born to her, because of the saying, "No moon, no man," which made her afeard every man-child she had. Do ye really think it serious, Mister Fairway, that there was no moon?'" Fairway replies: "'Yes; "No moon, no man." 'Tis one of the truest sayings ever spit out. The boy never comes to anything that's born at new moon. A bad job for thee, Christian, that you should have showed your nose then of all days in the month.'" [2]

In *South Moon Under*, when Lant is about to be born, the full moon is rising above the scrub. When one of the relatives predicts that Piety's baby will be a boy since there is a full moon, the old country doctor expostulates: "'I'll be dogged if I see how you womenfolks figure the moon when it comes to birthin' young uns. Don't none of you go that high to get one'" (57–58). So Lant enters the world on a full moon; and his cousin Cleve, who

is never much of a man (for all his having sired two children),
leaves the world when there is no moon.

III   *A Boy Becomes a Man*

Mrs. Rawlings put a great deal of herself into *South Moon
Under*. Lantry's wife, for example, is referred to as grumpy and
quarrelsome; she resembles the image that Mrs. Rawlings projected on occasion to those who came in contact with her. Moreover, the wife has much in common with the typical country-
woman in Mrs. Rawlings' fictions in that she is a stern, humorless
person with whom it is difficult to get along. Her daughter Piety
is very close to her father (much closer than any of her four
siblings)—as was the author.

But in Mrs. Rawlings' treatment of Piety's son Lant (an only
child) we see the ultimate expression of her alter ego, the dream
self that could *not* be actualized because she did not have a
little boy of her own. Lant Jacklin became her dream son, a
blurred sketch of what a boy of hers might have been like if she
herself had been a poor Cracker woman living in the scrub
country, like Mrs. Lantry, or like kindly old Mrs. Fiddia who did
have a son (cf. Grandmas Hutto and her son Oliver in *The Yearling*) and with whom she had lived for a brief period.

And in writing about Lant and his life in the woods Mrs.
Rawlings was clearly looking ahead to her magnum opus *The
Yearling*, which seems a fuller, more intense realization of this
early picture of the boy she never had.[3] Interestingly enough,
Jody Baxter's relationship with his father (in the latter book)
molds his life; but in *South Moon Under* Lant's father is a witless
incompetent and Lant's close ties are with his grandfather and his
mother. But in at least two passages describing Lant's experiences
with animals we find fragments of the yet-to-be-written *The Yearling*, passages which involve Lant's encounter with some wild
deer.

When Lant is eight, he finds fresh deer tracks not far from
his house, where the hammock growth borders the scrub clearing.
A seasoned woodsman, Lant identifies the tracks: a fawn and a
doe. There is no hint here of Lant's possible future attachment
to the fawn. Lant is now every inch the hunter; taking into
account how edible the fawn probably is now, the youngster is

eager for the kill. The three Lantrys—Lant, his mother and grand-father—follow the deer tracks into the scrub, and they find their quarry in an area of old pines. The fawn and doe are bedding: "The doe leaped up ahead of them. The fawn lurched to its feet and turned immense wondering eyes. Piety cocked her gun and levelled it; exerted her strength to pull the stiff trigger. She was slow. The fawn and doe were gone" (65). Significantly, the boy is furious with his mother for missing. (Mrs. Rawlings was, as I have reported, a bad shot; and near the end of *The Yearling*, Jody's mother's being a bad shot when she tries to kill his deer has other unfortunate results.)

When Lant is fourteen, he goes on a deer hunt in the hammock, near a swamp, to an area known as the Twin Sinks (these two sinkholes, otherwise insignificant in the story, prefigure the huge sinkhole not far from the Baxter cabin in *The Yearling*). It is south-moon-over, which to Lant means feeding time for the deer; and they suddenly arrive: "An old buck was there, leading the play, with a doe and a yearling. The buck ran down the far wall of the east sink-hole, then bounded up the near side, stretching his legs in the joy of the climbing. The yearling followed. . . . They raced and crowded one another. . . . Once the doe stood at the bottom with wary lifted head while the buck and yearling frolicked." But Lant has left his shotgun behind; much as he wants to kill them, he is powerless. Now follows a passage that belongs at the heart of *The Yearling*: "Yet the deer stirred him. If he had had his gun, he decided he would not have shot. They were strangely dear to him. They were a part of him, closer than his mother or his dogs or his bed" (108–09).

One of the misfortunes of Lant's life is that he did not ask Kezzy to marry him first, for he and the vivacious, winsome girl were strangely suited to each other; but, since he was two years younger than Kezzy and Cleve, he was, at the time they married, just getting out of his teens. Not only were the conditions inauspicious ones under which Lant and Kezzy finally united (Lant being her husband's killer), but a number of other events in Lant's young life help sustain the picture of Lant as a child of trouble.

His problems begin when Lant is a small boy, and his father (never much help around home under the best of circumstances) is killed in an accident. From this point on, Lant must assume the heavy responsibility of helping his mother, a frail and ineffective woman—and be the man in the family. Growing up in the near isolation of the backwoods, he lives through a number of lacerating experiences. There is the "Big Burn," a gigantic forest fire that threatens to wipe out much of the scrub, as well as the habitations of the scrub dwellers like Lant, his relatives, and their distant neighbors. Another difficulty is the closing of the "open range" by legislative act and the menace posed by a family of outlanders named Streeter to the local inhabitants who are able somehow to raise small herds of cattle on the coarse grass that grows in the scrub.

The Streeters uphold the state law—but violate local custom —by not allowing other people's cattle to range free over their land. Such a serious wrong, in the eyes of the economically depressed community (Lant's uncle Abner is particularly concerned), deserves an equivalent punishment. After a pointed warning, which is ignored, the Streeter men are taken from their houses one night by some of the local Crackers (including Lant) and given a severe whipping. Some time later Lant is arrested, and, although Abner posts bond for him, the boy is apprehensive about the impending trial; he faces imprisonment if he is found guilty of attacking the Streeters.

But Lant has more worries. Forced to earn a living for his mother and himself by whatever means are available, he has taken, in good Cracker fashion, to operating a hidden still in the woods. Good money can be made in this way, but he always faces the danger of discovery by "Prohis" (federal Prohibition agents), who are especially skilled at tracking down Cracker stills. Moreover, Lant's sweetheart, Ardis Mersey, is elusive and unaffectionate. It happens that she is related to the local game warden and that her family is connected somehow with the Streeters. Disturbed about Lant's uncertain future, she is waiting to see what happens to him before committing herself any further.

At the end of the story, which does not take Lant beyond the storm and stress of his emerging twenties, there are both dark clouds and silver linings. When the court trial over the Streeter incident is held, Lant is acquitted because of the faulty evidence submitted by the prosecution. But Ardis, who earlier had not seemed entirely trustworthy, seems less so now to him, and he severs their already tenuous relationship. And, before long, his treacherous cousin Cleve tells the "Prohis" about Lant's still, and they wreck it for him, which leads eventually to his killing Cleve and then (in effect) inheriting Cleve's wife and two small childen.

Stangely enough, considering the intense mood of the novel and the author's genuine dedication to her subject, most of the characters and events are described in such a low-keyed manner that a curious flatness exists throughout much of *South Moon Under*. Lant in particular is not adequately fleshed out. But one episode in his troubled career is memorably drawn: the river journey that he makes, when he is around eighteen, with another of the local characters.

In an effort to earn some money for himself and his mother, one dark and dreary fall (during a time when Cleve, useless and discontented, is living with them), Lant enlists the aid of Ramrod Simpson, a semidemented man with a cleft palate, a paralyzing phobia, and a great deal of river wisdom. Lant's plan is to salvage some cypress logs abandoned in a nearby creek and along the Oklawaha River landings not far away by a lumber processing firm. The idea is to raise the logs from the water—with log tongs and windlass—onto improvised scows and to crib-raft the logs east on the Oklawaha to its junction with the St. Johns River and then north on the St. Johns to the lumber mill at Palatka. (The going rate for such logs is twelve dollars a thousand pounds.) Old Ramrod, an excellent person in some ways if not in others for a partner in this kind of venture, has been logging by himself since the timber firm closed down its riverside operations.

Lant has been warned against working with the "crazy" Ramrod —legend has it that a baptizing preacher through carelessness almost drowned Ramrod in the Oklawaha, and then cracked his head on a rock in trying to get him out; hence his morbid fear of, and blasphemous attitude toward, Jesus Christ—but insists on doing it his way. When Ramrod agrees to the plan, Lant teams up with the foolish, unstable old man who is a public laughing-stock. Beautiful as the description of this river-journey is, it merely hints in the vaguest way at the rich, mythographic implications of such a trip: the (watery) open road for boys, the dangerous quest, the zone-crossing, the "holy union of males," and all the other symbolism detailed in the metaliterary criticism of Leslie A. Fiedler, Walker Percy, and other contemporary critics.

In what is perhaps the most unforgettable of all scenes, the boy becomes exhausted one day, towards sunset, and suddenly falls asleep. When he awakes, he is amazed to find the water lapping under the raft, which, gently rocking, is tethered around a bend in the river. He asks Ramrod what is the matter, having expected that they would continue to drift around the clock. Ramrod tells him, " 'You 'bout divv out. I been pushin' you. You belong to west. We dest camp tonight.' " Lant is embarrassed at having let himself go like that, but Ramrod says, " 'You dot to det used to this. You young. . . . You gwowin'.' " The old man runs his hand through his white hair and looks out over the black water. "He shook his head, trying to clear it of its confusion. He reached across his madness into a far past. He groped in a torment of remembering." Then, " 'I been a boy,' he said" (163).

At a number of points in this section of the story, the author rises to lyric heights, thanks partly to her peculiar sensitivity to "magic moments" when nature provided, somehow, a special heightening of awareness. "There came a time in mid-afternoon when all life seemed suspended. The river flowed interminably but as though without advance." Lant thinks he has always been in this fluid stillness. "There was no change . . . no memory and no imagining." His restiveness subsides. If his relatives "were really persons, instead of names, they lay drowned behind him. Nothing existed but the brown, clear water, flowing in one spot forever." The old man sits silently hunched over the sweep, "lunatic, insensate . . . The water lettuce whirled slowly around and around, like dancers waltzing in their sleep." The boy "watched until he drowsed with it; around and around and around" (163–64). At night, Lant, who likes "the swirling progress in the moonlight between the dark banks" (it is full moon), feels "the same drowsy excitement" that he knew when playing his grandfather's banjo. He observes limpkins and water-turkies far up in the cypress trees. Wood-ducks and herons, aroused by the noise of the raft, move away from their resting places. From the shore, owls too respond. Trees, clumps of river-grass, and shadow-laden banks go "by in the night like things remembered in a dream." The Oklawaha River flows, "a dream between dreams," and all are "one, the boy and the river and the banks." Lant is "conscious of lying immobile, borne resistlessly between two motions," that of the river below and that of the sky above (165).

Although Lant realizes a fair amount of money from the logs that he and Ramrod took to the lumber mill, Lant has to make two more river trips before spring. He does not mind, for he now feels more at home on the water than he does on land. The first of these additional trips passes without any comment on Mrs. Rawlings' part; but, on the last trip, something is wrong with the atmosphere, as far as Ramrod is concerned. Unnerved by the wind and the special quality of the air, he is frenziedly afraid that Jesus Christ will claim him at last. What with Ramrod's instability and a storm they encounter on the river, Lant fears that their sectional raft will pile up, which would be a genuine disaster. As weather conditions worsen and as Ramrod proves to be less and less reliable in helping to snub the raft around each bend in the river, it looks for a time as if the raft actually will pile up. Nothing goes right for the miserable pair. In the course of their misadventures on this unhappy journey, Ramrod loses his false teeth in the water, Lant almost drowns, and the food they took along is ruined in the storm. The author, in describing the boy's feelings, may once again have been voicing her own recurring insecurity: in Lant's view, the river was a betrayer; and when "familiar things" acted in this way, then truly was it "a bad matter" (173). After they finally reach Palatka, Lant and Ramrod find that the price of cypress logs has been cut—the crowning blow, it seems.

Precisely at this point in the story the author reveals what appears to be her extraliterary interest in Lant, whose development in the book is one more sensitive picture of the boy she never had. Worn out after all his tribulations—on the way back, his rowboat sprang a leak, and he has had a very long walk home—Lant undresses and goes to sleep in his bed. Piety is relieved that there will be no more rafting. Oddly enough to the outlander reader, Piety would not worry about his roaming freely in the scrub. No matter where he might travel, there—in Piety's view—the deadliest animal could not outdistance him. And in the scrub, neither darkness nor storm could make him go astray. But the river was another matter—it was not his element, and he had not the force to hold his own on it. Later, when he is rested and is able to tell her the sad story of the trip, she sits "rocking gently, watching him as though the sight of him fed a hunger" (174). A boy becomes a man, in the world of men. And, in the world of his mother, as Mrs. Rawlings surmised, he will always be something different from both, a source of spiritual nourishment that has never yet been named.

CHAPTER 3

Exile and Accommodation: *Golden Apples*

I "*Interesting Trash Instead of Literature*"?

DESPITE all the nerve-racking toil and care involved in writing her second novel, *Golden Apples*, Mrs. Rawlings was dissatisfied with the result. " 'I don't blame anyone but myself for *Golden Apples* being interesting trash instead of literature,' " she wrote to her Scribner's editor, Maxwell Perkins, on October 15, 1935. " 'But you should have bullied and shamed me further. I can do better than that and you know it.' " [1] To the anonymous reviewer in *The Nation, Golden Apples* was "given over to the staples of petty fiction," it was "trite and quite harmless." [2] "The people are disappointing," complained *The New Republic*,[3] but *The New York Times Book Review* was somewhat more favorable.[4] Mrs. Rawlings' literary executor, Julia Scribner Bigham, commented two decades later that *Golden Apples* was less successful than *South Moon Under*, "perhaps because the author had not the same distinctive sympathy with the main character, a young Englishman, that she had with the country itself and the Crackers." [5] Mrs. Rawlings' biographer, Gordon Bigelow, is generally disparaging in his remarks about the novel: "an ill-starred book from the beginning," "unity is so conspicuously lacking," etc.[6] Yet oddly enough, while she was revising the book for publication, the serial rights were sold to *Cosmopolitan* magazine, which wanted a shortened, four-installment version of the story.[7] And, during World War II, when the paper shortage was acute, the World Publishing Company published a hard-cover edition of the novel in its Forum Books series; this edition went through three printings between February, 1944, and April, 1946.

From the vantage point of the 1970s, Mrs. Rawlings' literary style, particularly her clumsy and unrealistic dialogue when she is not dealing with her familiar Crackers, weakens the book. The story itself is not so badly dichotomized as some have felt; her love for the Florida hammock and its inhabitants informs every page and enables her to convey her quasi-religious sympathy for the land with an emotional intensity that is easily perceptible by the reader. But, had Maxwell Perkins been more attentive to certain of her literary faults, she might have produced a novel which would have markedly advanced the reputation of the author of *South Moon Under* and the prize-winning story "Gal Young Un."

One of these literary faults has to do with the grotesquely unnatural speech of her non-Crackers, particularly the English-man Richard Tordell. Whenever he speaks, Tordell gives the impression of a computerized robot. For example, when his distant neighbor and fellow orange grower, the aristocratic Camilla Van Dyne, brings him some bud-wood for grafting, Tordell remarks, " 'But Mrs. Van Dyne, this is thoughtful of you. Brinley [his hired man] has been frightfully anxious about it' " (271). It takes very little effort to approximate what Tordell might really have said: "I say, that's awfully good of you, you know. My man Brinley has been in a perfect fever about it." When another acquaintance asks about the filly he has given Tordell, the latter replies, " 'She's a dear. I've ridden every day since I've been home' " (271). Another striking fault in *Golden Apples* is the odd tendency of the author to repeat the initial pronoun "he" throughout a paragraph describing a character's actions. Thus the strained quality of the writing becomes even more pronounced, and the reader grows increasingly discomfited as he sees the widening gap between what the writer wanted to do and what she actually managed.

These glaring gaucheries are difficult to explain in the mature, well-read Marjorie Rawlings, who was in the middle of her most productive period and was writing under almost ideal circumstances (so far as location and subject matter were concerned). But there is another, more subtle shortcoming in the author's manner of presenting her story: a painful literary naïveté, a glaring lack of dimensionality. *Golden Apples,* for all of its merits as a story of Florida life at the end of the nineteenth century, generally fails to capture our imagination. We miss such conventional literary devices as in-depth character analysis and the "iceberg effect"—revealing only a little and letting the reader discern the vast bulk of hidden meaning—so widely used by Hemingway.[8]

There are in the book, however, some very fine artistic touches that offset in part the noticeable deficiencies. For example, Luke Brinley's remarkable sermon on love (spoken to the aloof and indifferent Tordell, who has made Luke's sister Allie pregnant): " 'I been studyin'. A man kin love a woman a heap o' ways. He kin love her the way he love a drink o' likker on a cold evenin'. He kin love her hateful-like, the way a man that loves the taste o' quail-meat'll kill 'em in the nestin' season, jest so he gits the good of 'em hisself. Or he kin love her the way I'd be proud to figger you done loved Allie—gentle-like and lookin' out for her' " (260). There is also a beautiful passage about the bereaved Luke's grieving for his dead sister. Suddenly Luke is pricked by a thorn on the "small holly tree he had left to grow for Allie's pleasure. A hot hand seized his vitals. For an instant it was past bearing, that spring should be here, and the holly growing, and the sweet orange grove, and Allie gone past knowing (351–52)."

And, near the end of the book, there is a wonderful piece of uproarious humor worthy of comparison with the comic portion of William Faulkner's *As I Lay Dying*. Not long after Allie has died during pregnancy, Luke realizes that he must have a woman around to help with the chores and to do for him and Tordell, so he decides to get himself a wife right away. Whom does he choose but the mentally retarded daughter of a long-time acquaintance, a widow with a large brood of children. There is much comic dialogue here, as Luke woos the girl through her mother. (The point is made that love is not an issue in this business; Luke has no time for love now, especially after his beloved sister's death.) The widow Raynes expostulates with this Cracker Touchstone who is seeking his Audrey: " 'I mean, you figgered on it shore! I'll swear, Luke, this ain't decent. Courtin' and askin' and marryin' all in one day' " (334). But Luke will be served, and soon he and his "intended" and her mother ride off to the general store where the circuit riding preacher is expected to be (and, it is assumed, the storekeeper will stand treat).

Perhaps the author was mixing her modes somewhat too freely here: to describe Luke's sister's death, the story had just been pitched in a pathetic, poignant key. But it is hard to resist laugh-

ing at Mrs. Rawlings' graphic picture—sketched with flawlessly
appropriate dialogue—of the hurry-up, backwoods wedding and
the honeymoon in the kitchen. Luke doesn't want to waste a
moment, there is so much work to do. His newly wedded wife
explains that she has her best clothes on; Luke tells her bluntly,
" 'It ain't goin' to hurt 'em none to wash the dishes and scrub the
floor' " (337).

II   *The Spoils of Henry James: An Englishman in Florida*

Golden Apples, interestingly enough for a work by Mrs. Rawlings, suggests a basic Henry James theme: the confrontation of
European (Englishman) and American, a comparison of their
individual and national characters, and an assessment of the
relative merits of each—although, as stated earlier, the story lacks
in-depth character analysis. The central figure is a young English
gentleman from Hampshire, Richard Tordell. Through an unfortunate series of events, Tordell has disgraced himself with
his father; he resisted the blandishments of his father's young
wife—a latter-day Joseph ensnared by the consort of Potiphar—
who then denounced his "misconduct." As a result, Tordell is
banished forever; and he chooses to go to a remote part of the
Florida hammock land once occupied by an uncle of his. He is
to be sent a semiannual remittance by his father; otherwise, he is
completely divorced from family and homeland.

The dark, primitive, forbidding hammock of North-central
Florida—an entanglement of live oaks, magnolias, hickories, palms,
and sweet gums—is repugnant to Tordell, a nightmare fantasy
with which he cannot begin to cope. Questioned by a kind doctor
(who lives some distance away across the nearby Sawgrass Lake)
as to why he stays, Tordell candidly admits that he has no choice;
which is true, in the sense that he depends on his father for funds
and is incapable of earning his living by working. In a cruelly
direct rejoinder, Doctor Albury gives him a lesson in national
characterology: " 'That's where the American character has the
advantage over you Old World—decadents. An able-bodied young
man in this country never admits that he has no control over
his destiny' " (104)—a neat Jamesian touch.

Much of the story is devoted to portraying Tordell's weakness,
parasitism, aloofness, and general fecklessness, in contrast to the

fierce energy and resourcefulness of the hardy Cracker, typified by Luke Brinley—who is Tordell's age and height, almost a *doppelgänger* of Tordell—and his sister Allie. The title of the novel refers to the golden Florida orange, an embodiment of citric majesty which must be cultivated with painstaking care by dedicated growers such as Luke or the wealthy, aristocratic Camilla Van Dyne. The tendency of a displaced misfit like Tordell is merely to rail against his fate, admire someone else's golden orchard, ponder the symbolism of it all, and keep on drinking. Tordell muses over the golden apples of the Hesperides and the golden apple of Atalanta (remembering that *orange* was actually meant), losing "himself in antiquity. Here were ancient Greece and all of Persia. Here was old Seville. Here was Spain, starving, hoping, seeking, in Florida. Here were the magic isles, fruited with men's dreams" (236).

The story opens in the late nineteenth century with a double funeral in the heart of the virgin hammock land of Northern Florida. Luke's and Allie's parents are being buried in a clearing near the village of Purley,[9] and the youngsters (aged fourteen and ten) are left to fend for themselves. After several years (having survived numerous hardships), they move into the hammock land itself where there is an old deserted house in a little clearing adjacent to a grove of wild orange trees. Many years ago an Englishman named Tordell had lived there, but now Luke and Allie occupy the house. For the next four years they manage to eke out a bare living by growing sweet potatoes and corn, raising hogs and chickens, and cutting cypress into blocks and marketing it.

When young Richard Tordell arrives at the Florida hammock from Hampshire, England, to take over the long-neglected family estate, he allows the squatters to remain and work for him, and resigns himself to a life of desolation in the wilderness. Luke, bent on raising oranges (not the wild variety already growing there, but the "golden apples" that result from grafting and skillful cultivation), gets Tordell to let him work the orange grove. He also gets permission to seek expert advice from Camilla Van Dyne, who lives on the other side of the lake that lies not far away. Doctor Albury, who has developed a close interest in Luke, takes him to Mrs. Van Dyne's, where he will be obliged to remain for several weeks. By the time Luke returns, Allie has become Tordell's inseparable bedmate; before long she is pregnant. Tordell, contemptuous toward the Brinleys, is as indifferent toward what he has done as he is toward Allie's adoration and self-sacrificing compliance.

A long-time acquaintance of the Brinleys, the widow Raynes, tries to help the girl. When she realizes that Allie is no more than a trivial plaything to the "furriner," she sets the men of the nearby village to the task of exacting country justice. Thus, Tordell is savagely beaten in the middle of the night by a band of masked vigilantes. Luke finds the severely bruised body, and transports Tordell to Doctor Albury to be restored to health. When the Englishman recovers, Luke shames him into marrying Allie despite the fact that Tordell can barely tolerate the girl whom he has gotten with child. Aided by a gift of bud-wood from Mrs. Van Dyne for grafting onto the sprouts of the wild orange trees, and following her advice about burying the sprouts so that they will keep through the cold winter, Luke plans to develop a large, bountiful golden orange grove for his employer, who remains as indifferent to this project as he is to practically everything else.

Not long before the baby is due, Allie, who has been in poor health, suffers a fall, miscarries as a result, and dies. Then a severe freeze (actually, the famous Florida frost of 1895) wipes out all the orange crops, including Mrs. Van Dyne's; but Luke's buried sprouts survive. Later Luke takes the bud-wood and, with Tordell's aid, grafts it to the sprouts. With luck, there will someday be a magnificent crop of golden Florida "apples." Tordell, who has gone fox-hunting with Mrs. Van Dyne and her aristocratic friends from across the lake, and is willing to let his man Brinley fool around with the grove, attains contentment. "He thought, 'A good life—' " (347).

Thus we have a picture of the sturdy American, represented by Luke Brinley, a simple Florida Cracker. Energetic, resourceful, and unconquerable in spirit despite all adversity, he tames the wilderness and forces it to bear golden apples. And the idle, somewhat dissolute Englishman, who no longer has cause to bewail his outcast state, continues to indulge himself at others' expense—the Henry James story, with a vengeance? There is an added irony here, for Luke was the squatter, the trespasser, while Tordell was in a way the parasitized host. And the two men come eventually to form a symbiotic relationship, each one needing and feeding on the other. The author's sympathies are clearly with the American who has in a sense always been an "old man" (11) rather than a "new man," which was the way St. John de Crèvecoeur idealized the American, in the late eighteenth century.[10] Tordell, the "new man" (the alien intruder), must learn the meaning of life and human struggle from his elderly coeval.[11]

III   *"Love Is Not Enough. It Lets You Down."*

Golden Apples treats at length and in many different ways a very important subject of concern for Mrs. Rawlings: the over-riding importance of love and the seeming unavoidability of betrayal, after one gives oneself to love. Thus, Tordell says to Doctor Albury, who is nursing him back to health after his beating, "'You didn't agree with me once, Doctor, when I insisted that love was beastly, because it carried with it always, in one way or another, betrayal.'" Albury replies, "'I've had a great deal of love in my life, and sooner or later it's been a means of hurting me. I loved the woman who bore me, and she died. I loved the father who sired me, and he died. I loved the mother of my son, and she died, bearing him. I loved a woman again, and she went away and would have no more of me. All of it ended in pain.'" He concludes, "'I still say, I wouldn't have been without it. Not even to avoid the bitterness of death and betrayal, would I have done without the love'" (210).

There is obviously an inner core of heartfelt emotion on Mrs. Rawlings' part here. The passage recalls Charles Lamb's "The Old Familiar Faces" (1798): "I had a mother, but she died and left me"; "I loved a love once . . . Closed are her doors on me, I must not see her"; "All, all are gone, the old familiar faces." And there is also a suggestion of the notion that "'tis better to have loved and lost than never to have loved at all." On the highest level of literary representation, as in William Faulkner's "Beyond," this Tennysonian idea is transformed by an elderly judge who is mourning for his long-dead son into one of the most agonizing affirmations possible to man. If he could believe that he will see and touch his son again, the judge reasons, he will not have lost him; and if he has not lost him, he will never have possessed a son. He, the father, measures his own reality by these very experiences of death and bereavement. These provide immortality enough for him. In the context of an extraordinarily moving account of the judge's last hours on earth—as one part of his mind ventures beyond this world in search of the boy—this creed of love is a remarkable artistic achievement. The spirit of this utterance, if not the actual expression of it, is intimated in Albury's confession.

One major focus of this motif of "Love the betrayer" in the book is the relationship between Albury and his son Claude, a wild psychopath who can never find enough outlets for his hostility. It is ironic that, in Albury's recitation of his loves, he omits mention of his son, who is really the center of his life. When we first hear about him, the doctor has "a grown son, Claude, who ran wild and was the delight of his soul" (93). When he hears Claude coming home from one of his adventures, Albury says, " 'My son!' " The words are spoken with a deep "tenderness . . . to ease his heart in speaking them" (148). On another occasion when he hears Claude returning, Albury's "red face shone. He might have been a prophet awaiting his savior" (214).

This particular remark is interesting because it seems to transcend the fabric of the story itself. It might be compared with a passage in one of the best father-and-son stories of the 1960s, Bruce Jay Friedman's "23 Pat O'Brien Movies." In this story an elderly policeman, Officer Goldman, crawls out on a skyscraper window ledge to dissuade a distraught young man from jumping. Goldman listens to the man's troubles and then mentions his own, which are at least as bad: " 'I have one son and he's with his mother. Do you know what I think of him? It's like a religion and he's the one you're supposed to worship. He stays away from me like the plague.' " [12] Albury, whose own wife is dead, is in much the same position as the wifeless Goldman.

To compound the irony of Albury's situation, he has created a rationale about love. Love, as he tells Tordell, " 'is a multiplication. When you love, you're not alone. I love my son, and I blend myself with him. I'm more than myself. I am myself and I am also my son' " (212). He wouldn't trade his life for any man's, Albury insists: " 'And my people love me. They do love me, because love begets love' " (213). The man "was all father, and his brood, from his surly son through Tordell to his swarm of patients, returned him an impatient and sporadic affection, and laughed at him a little" (249).

In the course of the story Claude flies into a violent rage, beats a stallion that is in rut, and is trampled to death. Albury, strangely enough, receives the news somewhat stoically and is even able a little later to take a broad perspective on the matter. His son was mad, he admits to Tordell; but he, the boy's own father, couldn't face it because he loved Claude. " 'You don't know what it is—a man's love for his son.' " Tordell, who feels triumphant, longs to tell Albury, " 'Old man, you were vulnerable. Your love made you raw and defenseless.' " Then the doctor admits that he had spoiled his son, who " 'was never quite right.' " He comments, " 'You'd think love would make you wise, to do the wise thing.' " And Tordell thinks, " 'I was right. Love's not enough. It lets you down.' He wanted to say, 'There's nothing to fall back on but courage. You either have it or you don't.' He could not speak" (323). A neat Hemingway touch.

What apparently saves Albury from succumbing after his son's death is a fierce determination to extend his horizons of love. When Allie dies as a result of her fall, Albury pities Luke, feeling that it is foolish to pin our lives and hopes on a weak object, although we persist in doing so. Better, Albury indicates, not to give ourselves to one person or a few people, but to " 'all of life.' " In summation, Albury falls back on what the critic Kenneth Burke has called "socialization of losses" (reducing one's own sense of loss by taking the attitude that others are in the same boat)—in fact, socialization of grief and a kind of philosophical monism as well. "He said sternly, 'I should never grieve, Tordell, for my son. I should grieve for all men, tortured in living, finding their only peace in the enigma of dying— The maze of life, Tordell, the labyrinth of death— And it's probably all one, if we only knew——' " (329–30). In a cruelly ironic twist, Tordell *was* right: love would not be enough for Albury; it would let him down; but the kind doctor will probably always be able to fall back on some made-to-order philosophy about human relationships.

Another major focus of the "Love the betrayer" motif in *Golden Apples* is Tordell, who is inclined to make broad generalizations about human behavior. His young stepmother "framed" him, and his outraged father was unjust enough to banish him forever:

ergo, *love* equals *betrayal.* Thus, on originally arriving at the hammock (first having to cross a river called the Styx—an actual place name, incidentally), "he put the thought of England desperately from him, as usual, with a mingled hate and longing. He would allow himself to think of nothing with tenderness, because in all love, inherent, was betrayal" (87). Telling Albury about his past, Tordell laments, " 'I had the best. A life I wouldn't have changed for any other. Love, affection, loyalties, and all that. And the best betrayed me. What's left?' " Then, in his best Englishman-among-the-colonials manner, he points out, " 'I'm simply older than you, by years and years. I've found out the betrayal at the end of the road, that's all' " (110). Later, in a discussion with Albury about the advisability of multiplying oneself through love, abandoning oneself to another, Tordell reflects that these processes are precisely what had " 'cooked his goose' " in England and in Florida. " 'You love like a blind idiot, and you put yourself spotly in other hands, instead of staying safely in your own' " (223).

A third focus of this motif is Camilla Van Dyne. Her comments on love's betrayal assume particular significance in the light of certain aspects of Mrs. Rawlings' philosophy of life. The following conversation between Camilla and Tordell reveals the essential attitude of resignation and *caveat amator* that is associated with Mrs. Rawlings' life and work. The time is after Camilla has lost her orange crop in the big frost; Tordell envies her for having such a great love for her land that "not even its betrayal of her, its cosmic treacheries of drouth and killing cold, could alter the substance of her love." Camilla, crying silently, explains why she feels so bad—it's not the money that the crop loss represents. " 'It's the work all gone for nothing—as though children died—in some way you never expected them to die. The years you've watched the growing. You make them, you feed them, you love them. And overnight, they're gone.' "

Tordell understands her feelings—here Mrs. Rawlings is projecting herself into both sensitive characters—and he replies that what really hurts is the personal element: the individual's feeling that he alone has been selected from his fellowmen, over the long stretch of years, for a very particular and uncommon injury. Tordell stresses the horror a person feels in being betrayed. Camilla, of course, echoes these sentiments (which a reader of the 1970s, if not of the 1930s when the book appeared, would consider neurotic and paranoid). She admits that she has not expected a requital of proffered love from other people, and she implies that they cannot be depended upon. However, she had not anticipated this kind of treachery from something as salutary as her orange groves (308–09).

Who else in *Golden Apples* is betrayed by love or made to see the bitter irony of love's aftermath? There is Allie, who becomes a love-slave to Tordell. And there is her brother Luke, hoping to someday marry a woman he loves, delivering a sermon on love between a man and woman—and then taking for his wife a feebleminded girl whom he despises and mistreats. One of the shrewdest commentators on the whole subject is the widow Raynes. If Luke has no love for her daughter Bess, a lot of people marry without love, she points out; she and her late husband had been in love, but she isn't sure that they were more harmonious than unloving couples. And so Luke wants Bess now because he can't wait for true love to come along? As she sees it, he has already buried the only female he ever loved or ever will love.

IV *Affinities and Rejections*

Golden Apples is an intensely personal book in the sense that very many significant elements in it—besides the basic love and betrayal theme—are reflections of Mrs. Rawlings' own life and personality. In a revealing passage about Tordell's attitude toward the landed proprietors and professionals whom he has come to know, the author comments that he is as out of place with them as he would be with his own kind. Wherever he went, he would be, in effect, a foreigner. At one point she reveals her own social bias, attributing it to Tordell. Doubtless there were some individuals, naturally outgoing and preferring the urban life, who derived comfort from being with others like themselves; and they lived "like moles, in blindness to a natural background. While other moles, in numbers, tunnelled with them, they were content." As for Tordell, he knew he didn't belong to that group; privately, he "despised them" (249–50).

Again Mrs. Rawlings, in depicting Camilla, strikes the demophobic note that seems so uncalled for in the framework of her story. In a reference to maternity, we find Camilla preferring, somewhat improbably, to raise oranges rather than her own babies. When Albury compliments her on her orange trees, he adds the wry speculation that, if she had twelve children, she would certainly ignore the oranges. Gravely, she disagrees with this assessment: " 'People are slippery things to work with. I'm sure citrus is more satisfying. At least you're certain of your results' " (245). But this is not the *real* Camilla (or Mrs. Rawlings) speaking. At another point in the story, Camilla and Albury are regarding the pregnant and sickly Allie. Albury tells Camilla, who is hearty and robust, that *she* is really built for that sort of thing, and she says at once: " 'I'd be very glad to have it for her' " (296).

But the chief emphasis in the story is on the outlander Tordell, who comes to appreciate the appeal of the hammock land and orange groves. The author generalizes: "The relation between man and a natural background was profound. It completed him as no other human could complete him. . . . It would in the end absorb him. The dark earth would enfold him . . . his dust would be an indivisible part of it, earth and fog and palm and red-bird" (263). Later, talking with Camilla about the frost, Tordell realizes that "there were affinities between men and places, recognizable, so that a man lived contentedly wherever, by his nature, he belonged" (307).

In the end, Tordell genuinely accepts the land. Standing in the sand, he is filled with a deep contentment. (Mrs. Rawlings endows him with her own philosophy, with what Bigelow calls her "cosmic consciousness.") "It seemed to him that the inviolable pulse of the earth beat upward through his veins like sap. Nothing could strike him while he stood so joined to it. . . . When a man shaped growth to his ends, he put his hand on the secret core of creation . . . He joined himself to the earth, and because the earth itself was a little part of a farther universe, he joined himself through it to the stars, and in the union was his ecstasy" (351).

CHAPTER 4

"Give My Heart Ease, Love;
Give My Heart Ease":
The Yearling

I *Some Pictures of the Boy She Never Had*

PERHAPS the most important reason that *The Yearling* maintains so strong a hold on the reader is Mrs. Rawlings' profound sympathy for twelve-year-old Jody Baxter. Jody is a "natural" boy, not a *feminized* ideal of a boy: he is neither stereotypically good nor stereotypically bad.[1] But because the author is so attached to him emotionally he is virtually an *animus* figure in the Jungian sense: a projection of the masculine configuration of a woman's interior personality. Jody is Mrs. Rawlings' finest and most heart-warming literary expression of the boy she had always wanted but never had. All her life she had been describing this "dream child" in a variety of interesting ways, and she continued to do so long after completing Jody's story, but there is a special quality in *The Yearling* that sets it quite apart from those other works.

For a genuine appreciation of Jody as a living character of fiction, it helps to know what Mrs. Rawlings' other boy characters are like and, more important, the depth of her desire for a little boy of her own. Writing in 1940 to a friend from her undergraduate days at the University of Wisconsin who was then residing in London, Mrs. Rawlings remarked: " 'It is good that you have your son with you. I have often wondered if that relationship was not the most satisfying possible for a woman.' "[2] In the light of this statement and of her fictional treatment of the child-parent relation, it is fairly obvious that her solitary, rural life as a writer was basically unfulfilled but that it came closest to a qualified fulfillment when she could at least describe the having and nurturing of a young male child.

A very early foreshadowing of this deep need, possibly, is to be found in a story-note written when she was six. The contents of "The Bluebirds" were brief but to the point: "The mother bluebird married the father bluebird. They were very happy. The next day to their astonishment there were four little bluebirds in the nest." [3] Before long she had become the Story Lady of her Washington, D.C., neighborhood, entertaining the *boys* of her own age with stories by the hour.[4] Many years later, she recalled: "'As a child, I loved to tell stories. The other youngsters, in school and in church, discovered this streak of imaginative exhibitionism, and they used to ask me to spin yarns for them. But I used to select my audience. And in this selection I had but one rule. They *all* had to be boys. So anytime after Sunday School you could find me huddled on the steps of the church, dreaming it up under the inspiring gaze of my group of young male tall-tale addicts.'" [5]

Early in the 1910s, when she was fifteen and had been contributing for years to the children's page of various Washington, D.C., newspapers, she entered the Child Authorship Contest sponsored by *McCall's Magazine,* and won second prize, seventy-five dollars, for her story "The Reincarnation of Miss Hetty." Published in the August, 1912, issue of *McCall's,* the story is about an aged spinster named Miss Hetty Simpkins, whose only brother had drowned while still a very young man (both parents were dead). One day a small dirty boy from the local orphan asylum calls on her and tries to sell her a dog; she refuses him curtly. Later she thinks better of it and, wanting to make amends, recovers the boy and takes him home with her. Sometime later, after he has been put to bed for the night, she discovers that he has the manner, in his sleep, of her long-dead, golden-curled brother.[6]

At the time young Marjorie Kinnan wrote this short sketch she had a younger brother, Arthur (the only sibling she would ever have), who was born when she was about four. In "The Reincarnation of Miss Hetty" she was apparently transferring her deep fondness for little boys to her brother and, at the same time, projecting a mother-son relationship for the two of them. There is something peculiarly noteworthy in this simple tale, the principle of prefigurement; but discussion of this factor must be deferred for the present.

While an undergraduate at the University of Wisconsin from 1914 to 1918, she continued her literary efforts and was very active in the "creative" movements and organizations on campus. In the light of this discussion, one of her undergraduate poems is extraordinarily revealing. Even the title she chose for it says a great deal about her inmost feelings. The poem follows:

"The Miracle" by Marjorie Kinnan [7]

I lay with half-closed eyes, worn out with pain;
And day was night, and life a fearful thing.
I heard a stirring, as of flowers in rain,
Or little birds that move before they sing.
And by my side I found a fairy form,
"Your own. A sturdy son," the kind nurse smiled.
A bundle of pink rose-leaves, soft and warm—
And unbelievable! A mystic child!
The white-garbed angel placed it close to me,
Showed tiny face and dimpled fingers bared,
And smiled again, and "Hush"-ed mysteriously;
Then tip-toed 'round the room. And still—I stared!

*   *   *

In dashed an interne with a tragic face.
"My God!" he cried. "My God! What have you done?
The infant here? This girl's a tonsil case!
It goes to Mrs. B—, in forty-one!"

In the later 1920s, when she had become Mrs. Rawlings and was spending much of her time as a journalist and as a free-lance fiction writer (entirely without success), she wrote a series of short poems, "Songs of the Housewife," dealing with the "romance of pots and pans." These homey little verses, bearing such titles as "Envy" and "Ancestral Pies," were syndicated in the *Rochester* (New York) *Times-Union* and other Gannett newspapers. One of the "housewife songs," "Unseen Visitors," strongly suggests a maternal yearning. Following are the first and last stanzas:

Who tiptoes through my house when I am gone?
The door's no sooner locked than I can hear

A rustling, as of footsteps on the lawn,
  And unseen figures moving past my ear.

*   *   *

I like to think they are my loved ones lost,
  Come back a moment when the house is hushed.
And that some ghostly part of me plays host
  There in the rooms their souls, refreshed, have brushed.[8]

Another instance of blighted motherhood occurs in her prize-winning story of 1931, "Jacob's Ladder." A young Cracker girl, Florry (the character was based on the wife of Mrs. Rawlings' grove man, described in chapter 7 of *Cross Creek*), who, after enduring extreme privation, loses her small baby, is a strikingly portrayed sorrowing mother. In her bereavement-grief she seizes upon a baby coon as a substitute, but her husband will not let her keep the animal. At one point in the story, she looks yearningly at a little boy and girl belonging to a Yankee farmer, watches them with dismal longing, and thinks how, if they were hers, she would make them come in out of the heat.

When we briefly review Mrs. Rawlings' novels, we find that her first book, *South Moon Under* (1933), is about a Florida Cracker woman, Piety Jacklin, and her beloved only son, Lant. The second novel, *Golden Apples* (1935), which has a great deal to say about maternity and child-parent relations, contains a subplot about a widower who worships his scapegrace son and then must endure the son's senseless death. *The Yearling* (1938), as will soon be shown, is an unusually moving story of the closeness that is possible between a father and his son; aside from the Baxters, there are two other family groups (the Huttos and the Forresters) in which a beloved son plays an important role. The last novel, *The Sojourner* (1953), is essentially the story of an *unwanted* son who must abide his mother's single-minded dedication to his long-absent brother, as well as the griefs his own children bring him. This last work is also a veritable maze of parent-offspring relationships, natural and artificial.

A strange little story called "The Pardon" appeared in the August, 1934, issue of *Scribner's*. Recalling elements and situations in an old Wessex tale by Thomas Hardy and in Faulkner's early novel *Sanctuary* (1931), "The Pardon" deals with a prisoner in the penitentiary who is unexpectedly pardoned and returns home to find one more child than he knew he had waiting for him. Guiltily, the wife explains that she couldn't manage the farm alone; she did not expect that he would be pardoned; etc. Now desolate and estranged from his wife and daughters, the returned convict spends his first night at home lying very reluctantly on a narrow bed by the side of his wife's four-year-old son. " 'Pore little bastard,' he said, 'I reckon you wasn't much wanted.' " When the child cries out in fright, the man comforts him: " 'Running from the booger-man, sonny?' he asked. 'Don't you fret—I've got a-holt of you.' " [9] In this artless tale we find echoes of the anecdote that the author had written at fifteen, "The Reincarnation of Miss Hetty": the dependent or suppliant little boy; his rejection by a potential parent-figure; the latter's change of heart; and the forming of new (kinship?) ties. The stone which the builders rejected is become the head of the corner.

In 1936, while Mrs. Rawlings was working on *The Yearling* at a retreat in Banner Elk, North Carolina, an odd thing happened to her which intensified her long-unfulfilled hunger for a boy of her own. The incident also caused her to write a half-autobiographical story which she later expanded into a novelette that was serialized in *The Saturday Evening Post* but, justifiably, was never reprinted in book form or anthologized. Not far from where she was staying in the Carolina mountains was an orphanage, and, in the course of her sojourn at Banner Elk, Mrs. Rawlings came to know one of the inmates, a twelve-year-old boy named Dale Wills. Something about the boy—his strength of character, his wistful expression, his unique manner, perhaps—made a profound impression on her (let us recall her "Reincarnation of Miss Hetty" again). As she worked on her novel about a lonely twelve-year-old boy named Jody Baxter, her protagonist's real-life counterpart, so to speak, took on the luster of an imperishable ideal. Dale was apparently the kind of boy that Mrs. Rawlings could visualize as the son she'd never had, and she thought seriously of adopting him. While nothing came of this idea, they maintained correspondence: she heard from him two or three times a year until World War II, after which the letters ceased. In the late 1940s she discovered that he was alive and well, married in fact, his navy days now far behind her.[10]

Aside from Dale's part in inspiring the short story "A Mother in Mannville" (*The Saturday Evening Post*, December 12, 1936), and the six-part novelette *Mountain Prelude* (*The Saturday Evening Post*, April 26, 1947, to May 31, 1947), he seems to have had no other important effect on Mrs. Rawlings, despite all the deep emotions he once stirred in her. Bigelow, who in his biography of Mrs. Rawlings touches too casually, I believe, on her frustrated maternal instincts, was doubtless referring to Dale when he wrote the following: "She often regretted being childless, though not in the fashion of some women [whose entire lives are] darkened by a sense of irretrievable loss. She was particularly fond of little boys, more so than of girls, and on two occasions came within a breath of adopting a son, but was deterred in one case by entanglements with the boy's family, in the other by religious considerations raised by officious bureaucrats." [11]

"A Mother in Mannville" and its expanded version, *Mountain Prelude*,[12] are both dream stories arising from the author's most cherished but unrealizable longings. "A Mother" is by far the better of the two, but the unbelievably poor writing of *Mountain Prelude* is probably not to be explained as casually as Bigelow would have us believe: "This was pure hack-work, a pot-boiler which Marjorie turned out almost cynically, too deeply involved now in the rat race of the big-time to be able to say no to the sixty thousand dollars it netted her." [13] The subject was too intimately a part of her psyche for her to be anything like cynical about it; but how are we to explain the lapse in literary judgment that the story represents?

Mrs. Rawlings seems to be speaking in propria persona, in the first-person narrative "A Mother in Mannville." She was in the Carolina mountains one autumn to be alone so that she could "do some troublesome writing." Needing someone to take care of her chores, she applied at the nearby orphanage; and a twelve-year-old boy named Jerry answered her call. Jerry, who had been at the orphanage since he was four, was unbelievably lovable; and he was also highly skilled at woodchopping and at the other tasks she assigned him. He made his way directly into her heart and speedily gained the devotion of her pointer, Pat: ". . . it seemed to me that being with my dog, and caring for him, had brought the boy and me, too, together, so that he felt that he belonged to me as well as to the animal." [14] Jerry told her about his mother, who lived in Mannville (he would later discuss with the narrator his plans for buying his mother a gift with what he had earned), and she became extremely upset at the thought of a mother who could leave a son like Jerry in an orphanage for so many years. When it came time for her to leave for home, she wanted to say good-bye to Jerry, who had served her so self-sacrificingly. But, she was told by one of the orphanage officials, Jerry had become ill and had gone off someplace by himself. And, when the narrator asked about that mother of his, she was informed that Jerry had no mother. *Here the story ends.*[15]

If we set aside for a moment the core of *Mountain Prelude* (essentially that of "A Mother"), what remains is a string of wild improbabilities which clearly was not ready for publication in a national magazine. But how much it reveals about what was really going on in Mrs. Rawlings' mind all of those years! Since the entire plot does not bear repeating, only the really significant story elements will be considered. Pieced together, in the light of our thesis about Mrs. Rawlings' pictures of the boy she never had, they constitute a remarkable study of a woman's tormented mind fantasizing dream children and redemptive second chances.

The heroine is Helen Jackson, a widow who happens to be a concert pianist. Her husband, Major Hank Jackson, had been killed in an air battle; and she is left with only her *twelve-year-old son*, young Hank. The boy hates music but loves airplanes. One day he finds a plane on a nearby golf course; the keys happen to be there too. Hank takes the plane up for a spin; the plane crashes; Hank is killed. Helen is so devastated that she is unable to function, and even her music is impossible for her now. The doctor advises her, " 'You're not the only woman to whom tragedy has come. Other women face it.' " She replies that she can't help herself—she is frozen. The doctor understands. " 'You feel that you can't bear any sort of human contact. Is that true?' " Yes, Helen answers: " 'Especially children. I'm afraid of what I may do the first time I see a woman with a boy—a boy about twelve.' " [16]

With her faithful dog Jock, Helen escapes in her car to the remote Appalachians. In the isolated hamlet of Brushy Gap she finds an empty cottage for rent *with a baby grand piano in it too* and decides to settle here for a time. No one is near to ask questions; no reminders are present; they must have been headed this way from the beginning, she tells her dog.

The proprietor of the local grocery, Mr. Williegoode, supplies her with the things she will need. The mountain children, curious to see what this strange outlander is like, cluster around her car, but she cannot stand their presence and sends them away angrily. But she will need someone to do certain chores, and a mountain boy named Jerry applies for the job. He is the very size and age of her dead son Hank (a perfect *doppelgänger* in fact), and he and Jock make friends at once. Unable to stand the sight, Helen flees to the bedroom, shuts the door, throws herself on the bed, and sobs brokenly. When Jerry leaves, she again shuts "the door against the boy and the world." Later Mr. Williegoode (who is only one of the many guiding lights in the story) reproaches her for chasing away the mountain children. When she explains that she just can't stand children around her, and apologizes, he warns her—"'Well, ma'am, they's a heap of young 'uns in the world. You'll be hard put to it to keep away from 'em.'" [17]

From her mountain retreat Helen writes letters to her close associates. To her concert manager, Arthur Norton (note: Arthur was the name of Mrs. Rawlings' only brother; Norton, the name of her second husband), she says that it will be a long time before she really plays again, and that she will not compose any more. She also mentions the mountain boy who had come to help her.

Throughout *Mountain Prelude* there are a number of psychological touches that clearly indicate the author's depth of feeling for Jerry (who is a reincarnation of Helen's dead son, one gathers; cf. "The Reincarnation of Miss Hetty") and her characteristic mode of thinking. But for some reason these elements are treated so carelessly that they serve to detract from an already weak tale. For example, Helen unintentionally rebuffs Jerry, who has used the dollar she paid him to buy himself a harmonica and her dog Jock a rubber ball. Jerry is asked why he did not enter her cabin through the front door, and he answers that he hadn't been invited. Whereupon Helen is overcome with a desire to tell him to come in at any time by either door. Then Helen plays a piano accompaniment to a mountain tune Jerry renders on his harmonica—and they make beautiful music together. She takes Jerry for a ride in her roadster, and he is filled with joy at the idea of being with her and the dog—as though they were a family.

In the neighboring town of Minton, Helen enjoys a reunion with another of her mentors, the famous pianist Jacques Dumond.

They discuss her composition, "American Fantasy," and Mr.
Dumond gives her some advice about fantasy, suffering, and the
beneficial effect of the latter on the music she will someday
write. Then he sums matters up for Helen (and apparently for
the author, too) by saying, " 'Dear Helen, when you are as old
as I, you will discover that the human heart is a stout thing.
You can drop it and break it in a thousand pieces, over and
over again, and love will put it together better than new. Go
back to your work now, and do not close any doors.' " [18]

Mountain Prelude moves rapidly now through a series of
amazing developments. Young Jerry gets pneumonia from being
out in the rain while taking care of Helen's dog. At once she
begins nursing him back to health and is joined in this mission
by a neighbor, the wounded war veteran Bill Chandler. Through
Bill's encouragement (he lends her a cookbook), Helen begins
cooking for the first time in her life. (See the "Our Daily Bread"
chapter in *Cross Creek*, and *Cross Creek Cookery*.) After Jerry
recovers, Helen and Bill are invited to a fox hunt in the mountains.
They discuss this hunt, and Bill tells her that she and the boy
" 'belong together. You should adopt him. You're dodging life.
It's understandable, because of your tragedy, but you can't escape
forever.' " [19]

Not long afterward Helen's dog smells smoke, and he leads
Helen and Bill back to the orphanage, which is on fire. Jock finds
the sleeping Jerry and wakes him; then boy and dog save all of
the orphans. Since the orphans are now homeless, each of the
hunters in the fox hunt takes several children home; Helen is to
take Jerry. At this point in the story, Jerry tells Helen about his
"mother" who lives in Mannville, and there is a brief recap of
the original short story.

When Helen receives a telegram from her manager, Arthur
Norton, saying that he wants her to give a piano recital in San
Francisco for five thousand dollars, she plans to accept the offer
and use the money to rebuild the orphanage. Bill, who has been
reproaching Helen for not recognizing that Jerry wants her to
be his mother, says, " 'Dear Helen, don't you know that you take
nothing away from the dead when you love again? Does it deprive
your own lost son of love, to give a share to Jerry?' " [20] Finally,
Helen is persuaded to become a mother to Jerry. However, Bill
Chandler has already put through adoption papers for the boy,

and so Helen will have to take him too, if she really wants Jerry; and she agrees to do so. Jock is also included in the arrangement, and, as the tale ends, the four principals are about to form one big happy family. Once more Mrs. Rawlings' imagination addressed itself to the stone which the builders rejected.

The other remaining stories in the "dream child" group are hardly less embarrassing or revealing. Aside from the bothersome question of how her very worst writings managed to achieve publication (and sometimes even additional recognition), there remains the paradox of a skilled writer who dedicated her life to writing serious fiction, but often turned out mere wish-fulfillment fables or poorly contrived narratives with protruding authorial wishes.

"In the Heart" (*Collier's*, February 3, 1940) is a fictional account of some complicated events, involving the author's Negro helpers on her orange grove property, that later appeared in extended form in the "Black Shadows" chapter of *Cross Creek*. All that matters here is the narrator's comment at the end of this artless and tasteless story of an ugly Negro who is rejected by everyone, black and white, and who has only one aim in life, to make things grow from the soil. Black Bat, as he is called, is nearly killed in a shooting, but he recovers and returns to the narrator's garden to be with his beloved plants. "'I stared at his hands,'" the narrator says. "'They were the hands of a black father, cradling the helpless children of the earth.'" [21]

"The Provider" (*Woman's Home Companion*, June, 1941), like several other stories of hers, features a would-be father figure instead of a quasi-mother figure. The setting is not the North Florida backwoods but the Georgia pine country. The protagonist is Big Joe, an unmarried railroad fireman who has a soft spot in his heart for children. Two youngsters in particular have caught his fancy, and he has a deep urge to give them presents and lumps of coal as he rides by in his locomotive. Big Joe is fired for illegally giving away the coal from the tender, and he returns to where the two children's house is located. But, he finds, they and their mother (they have no father) have gone away. But where? Then he discovers an envelope, belonging to them, from a rural route in Alabama. And so he leaves at once to try to find "his people," going "southward in the sunset." [22]

"Black Secret," the 1945 *New Yorker* story which won Mrs.

Rawlings another O. Henry award, is about a seven-year-old white boy named Dickie Merrill, who lives in a Southern city at the turn of the century; he discovers that his great-uncle, like other prominent white men of the community, has had sexual relations with a Negro woman (the "black secret"). The revelation makes little Dickie ill, and the conclusion of the story focusses on the disruptive effect of this discovery on Dickie's health. True, we are shown a close mother-son relationship, but it is treated with such garish sentimentality as to make the entire piece seem, today, like a carelessly handled travesty. The writing, particularly of the dialogue, is unbelievably bad; and one of the most incredible features of this story is its having been published at all (even in *The New Yorker*), its winning an O. Henry prize, and its being reprinted in two anthologies.

Last, there is the January 1, 1949, *Saturday Evening Post* short-short, "The Friendship," a tale about a six-year-old boy named Robert Wilkinson. One day Robert falls down, cries in pain, and is helped home by a kind policeman, Sergeant Masters. They discuss Robert's mother, and Masters tells Robert how lucky he is: " 'I didn't have a mother when I was your age.' " Robert was under the impression that everyone had a mother. *They do, at the beginning,* Robert is told. " 'But sometimes a mother can be lost.' " Then Robert asks if the sergeant has a little boy of his own. " 'No, Robert, I should have liked a dozen, but I shall never have a single one.' " Robert asks how he can know this. " 'Sometimes . . . it is possible to know.' "

Robert gives his protector some windfall apples from his yard, and a fast friendship develops between the two; Sergeant Masters makes it his business to meet Robert after school every day to walk him home. Soon, however, Robert (who thinks the kind officer is being paid to escort him home), begins to take advantage of the man. Resenting the fact that two neighbor children (who have no apple tree of their own) have been taking his windfall apples, he tells on them and asks Sergeant Masters to arrest them. The police officer, outraged at Robert's conduct, his abuse of their friendship, is ready to sever his relationship with Robert at once. The terrified boy clasps Sergeant Masters in desperation, and he is forgiven by the understanding officer. Robert is made to realize that he had violated the social code—a harsh lesson indeed for a spoiled six-year-old whose "mother was often unduly solicitous"—but all's well that ends well.[23]

These basic story elements—the little lost boy, the parental-wish fulfillment, the rejection of the child corrected by acceptance and reunion—combine again to reveal what happened to Mrs. Rawlings' writing when she was apparently receiving no inspiration whatever from people, places, and things. Drama is turned into caricature, soul-heavings are distilled into bathos, and a formidable gap exists between private fantasy and public art, or even popular literature.

But, in Thomas Hardy's words (from "In Tenebris II"), *if way to the Better there be, it exacts a full look at the Worst*. What was lacking in Mrs. Rawlings' shorter fictions about real or fancied parenthood, what was touched on sketchily or with moderation in her other novels, was treated with consummate artistic skill in her finest book, *The Yearling*, which more than makes up for her weak and uninspired writings. By no means only a well-executed story about a father and son, or a boy and his pet deer, *The Yearling* has a kind of mythical quality which repays each successive reading. This novel elevates the writer to the rank of those special authors who at least once in their lives are capable of giving us dreams to dream by and words to shape those dreams.

II The Yearling: A Boy and His Book

The enormous popular success of *The Yearling*, which was published in April, 1938, is a commonplace of twentieth-century publishing history in this country. Consider its triumphs: Book-of-the-Month Club selection, movie rights sold to Metro-Goldwyn-Mayer, best-seller status, Pulitzer Prize, global acclaim, and—best of all, perhaps—the currency of a household word. But serious literary critics have tended to disparage Mrs. Rawlings' achievement in *The Yearling* or to neglect it altogether.[24] Seeming to lack the mythic or at least the suggestive elements of American classics such as Nathaniel Hawthorne's *The Scarlet Letter*, Stephen Crane's *The Red Badge of Courage*, Mark Twain's *Huckleberry Finn*, Herman Melville's *Moby-Dick*, and William Faulkner's *The Bear* (despite the great bear hunt that means so much to Jody and Penny Baxter), *The Yearling* has never been given the critical recognition it deserves.

In June, 1933, Mrs. Rawlings' editor, Maxwell Perkins, suggested a story about a child living in the scrub woods.[25] On October 27, 1933, he wrote: "I am thinking of a book about a boy, but his age is not important. Every boy between twelve and eighteen who lives an outdoor life is interested in the same things." Perkins had in mind certain well-known books designed primarily for boys but also read by men: *Huckleberry Finn*, Rudyard Kipling's *Kim*, David Crockett's *Memoirs*, R. L. Stevenson's *Treasure Island*, Edward Eggleston's *The Hoosier School Boy*. He noted that "the best part of a man is a boy. It is subject matter that counts, and the fact that the hero is a boy." And "a book about a boy and the life of the scrub is the thing we want." Other things were wanted too, Perkins made clear, such as some of the important elements she had put into *South Moon Under*: "those wonderful river trips, and the hunting, and the dogs and guns, and the companionship of simple people who care about the same things." She was not to overlook the river journey because "the rivers there are so good, and the journey element in a narrative is always a fine one, particularly to youth." Casually, Perkins commented, "It is all simple, not complicated—don't let anything make it complicated to you." [26]

Ironically if not perversely, Mrs. Rawlings was slow to respond to a suggestion that should have called forth her deepest emotions. She had another literary project on her mind, the story of an Englishman in the Florida hammock country. In the latter part of 1933 she did two things calculated to further that project. One, she made a brief trip to England in order to absorb the atmosphere so that her Florida Englishman could be developed realistically. (As it turned out, he never was.) And, she returned for a time to the scrub country to live with the family of Cal Long, an elderly hunter "whose father shortly after the Civil War had homesteaded a plot of ground in the scrub when it was still an unspoiled wilderness." [27]

She wrote eagerly to Perkins that she hoped he could someday see Mr. Long's old place in the heart of the scrub country (his home since 1872), "falling into decay under the exquisite mantle of flowering vines. They are hard put to it to make a living, principally because the deer and foxes eat their crops almost faster than they can raise them. They are in the forest preserve and are not allowed to kill game." Mrs. Long, when asked by her prospective guest what she should bring along, chucklingly replied, " ' "Something to eat." ' " [28] But for some reason, this visit was unproductive. " 'Do you realize,' " she asked Perkins, in reply to his letter of October 27, 1933, " 'how calmly you sit in your office and tell me to write a *classic?*' " [29]

Perkins was as reassuring as ever as he encouraged her to give top priority to the "novel" if she wished. He did not want to hurry her writing on either project, but one of his reasons for suggesting the boy's book was his feeling "that having done so well by Lant [the young protagonist of *South Moon Under*], and having thought so much about the scrub, and the rivers, and alligators, and all, from the point of view of Lant, you would be pretty well primed for a book about another boy. But it is all right that you should do the way you think best." [30] This letter was written on November 15, 1933. Something like two years was to elapse before she would return to this task. The "novel," *Golden Apples*, apparently had to be completed first; it was published in 1935.

At the outset, as she wrote Perkins in the fall of 1935, she still lacked enthusiasm for the job: not enough material. (Did she mean not enough inspiration?) Then she scrawled him an excited note. The right feeling for the boy's story had finally come to her. It would be " ' 'a brief and tragic idyll of boyhood' " and about fifty thousand words long. [31] Now her raw data, her experiences, her environment, would be working with her instead of against her.

And so Mrs. Rawlings drove back to the pine clearing where the elderly hunter Cal Long had lived ("Pat's Island"), and it now became Penny Baxter's clearing in her new story. With Mr. Long dead, the clearing in the tall pines impressed her more than ever before because of its isolation and silence; and the huge, funnel-shaped hole not far from the dilapidated, abandoned house suggested interesting possibilities. In July, 1936, she met Barney Dillard, another elderly hunter who had also lived for years in the scrub country; and he was willing to share with her his vast fund of hunting stories and wilderness lore. He even took her with him a number of times when he went bear hunting. [32]

Now full of enthusiasm for her literary materials, she was

optimistic about what could be done with them. The finished product would not be a mere long story but a full-length novel. And she wrote Perkins, " 'the short narrative I had in mind will make my culminating point—my climax and my point, and a very stirring point it is, too. It will be absolutely all told through the boy's eyes. He will be about twelve, and the period will not be a long one—not more than two years. I want it through his eyes before the age of puberty brings in any of the other factors to confuse the simplicity of viewpoint. It will be a book boys will love . . .' " [33] Perkins, in his reply on August 5, 1936, gave her more reassurances and expressed his high hopes: "I have the most complete confidence in the quality of this book. I would not be a bit surprised if it were the best book you have done, and it might well be the most successful." [34]

(Despite her feelings about small boys, and maternity, it is hardly surprising that Mrs. Rawlings had not immediately seen the possibilities in doing the kind of book that Perkins had suggested. There is always the danger of a writer's being too close to a cherished subject to do a proper job with it—a danger to which Mrs. Rawlings succumbed after her success with *The Yearling*. But, as many can testify, if a writer is somehow lucky enough to get the "right feeling"—which passeth understanding—the base metal of experience and wishing can indeed be transmuted into artistic gold.)

Thoroughly involved with her ever-developing *bildungsroman*, Mrs. Rawlings did a strange thing. She left Cross Creek (the time was early September) and sought refuge in the Carolina mountains. Renting a cottage near the village of Banner Elk, North Carolina, in a high, beautiful mountain valley, she surrendered herself to Jody Baxter and his problems. For almost three months she remained in this new and deeply gratifying paradise of isolation,[35] boarding with a Miss Fannie Lowe [36] and writing, writing in a way that might not have been possible had she remained at home. Here she received an unexpected benefit in the form of the little orphan boy described in the short tale "A Mother in Mannville," and in a later elaboration of it, the novelette titled *Mountain Prelude*. Thus the real boy, Dale Wills —mentioned earlier in this chapter—and his world merged in a sense with her dream-child, Jody Baxter, and became part of *his* world.

Perkins, writing to Mrs. Rawlings on December 13, 1937, after he had read the completed manuscript, began by saying that he had read the entire book "with constantly growing interest." He thought the last half was better than the first. Moreover, "the book gets increasingly good." However, "the very beginning now is perfect, it seems to me, and of course the father and mother, and all about that life, and Jody's on the island, are as good as can be." Among the suggested changes Perkins ventured were these: Mrs. Rawlings might make the toughness of the Forresters clearer to the reader, cut out the next-to-last paragraph, and "cut out the unseemly performance of the old lady . . ." (Mrs. Rawlings must have done so, for, of the small number of old or middle-aged ladies in the book, not one acts in an unseemly manner; yet, how could Perkins, who was so concerned with public taste as well as with book sales, have countenanced the blasphemous Ramrod Simpson in *South Moon Under?*) Perkins concluded, "It is a very beautiful book, and I greatly enjoyed every minute of it. Otherwise I would have read it faster. The better a book is, the slower I go." [37]

As for the precise setting of *The Yearling*, a recent article in the naturalists' magazine *Audubon* is extremely helpful. That part of the "Rawlings country" where most of the action of *The Yearling* occurs (the scrub) is east of Ocala, southeast of Gainesville, and east of the north-south freeway. Here are "rivers and lakes and crystal springs bubbling up from the underlying limestone aquifer . . . [geologists call] the Ocala dome—the largest single water storage in the United States. It is a country of orange groves, hugging the lakes as insurance against frost; of stock farms with hundreds of acres of neatly fenced pasture, here and there shaded by great live oaks; of hardwood hammock (a few virgin stands remain); of pineland and scrub forest, famous for its abundance of game . . . [which] flourishes in Ocala National Forest . . ." This region, roughly twenty by forty miles in surface area, is bordered by the Oklawaha River on the west and by the St. Johns River on the east.[38]

According to Bigelow in *Frontier Eden*, the "pine island" where the Baxters lived ("Pat's Island" in actuality) was "about two miles west of Silver Glen Springs which rises near the shore of Lake George." Cal Long's old homestead, which served as a model for the Baxters', was "a cypress-shingled frame house and barn and smokehouse with about thirty acres of cleared ground surrounded by split rail fence and located close to a great limestone sink where seepage provided the chief source of water." Among the other landmarks that Mrs. Rawlings used are: "Juniper Springs a few miles to the south with its creek which runs through dense forest before breaking out into a marshy, green valley and emptying into Lake George; Salt Springs, ten miles to the northeast; the frontier trading posts of Ft. Gates and Volusia on the St. Johns." [39]

More importantly, perhaps, *The Yearling* was set in a magic moment of experience—a kind of secular epiphany, involving the writer herself, as a child—and in harmony with the universe. She was in harmony, yet all too painfully aware of fleeting time, of the sadness that lies at the core of existence and somehow must always be borne. At the time of this experience, she was ten years old, and it was April: Chaucer's April, with its sweet showers and nature pricking in the hearts of the small birds; and T. S. Eliot's April, "the cruellest month." Mrs. Rawlings described that April moment to a journalist who was doing a feature story about her for *The Family Circle*:

"One of those April days so beautiful you want to reach out and hold it so it will not move on and die. I was standing under a tree. The sun shone through the leaves and a soft breeze caused the light and shadow around me to shift and change. There was a stillness. A stillness that was like the stillness the day Father died. [He died early in 1913, when she was sixteen.] And with it came a feeling of ecstasy and regret—a lifting sensation but tinged with sadness. It was a definite premonition of maturity. . . . Through the years the thought of that April day, instead of becoming a dim memory, became more insistently poignant. I had thought of doing a short sketch based on the impression. This was stretched to a short story. Then, when I moved to Florida, the full significance of that premonition of maturity came to me, and I wrote 'The Yearling.' " [40]

Some years later, in a radio talk for a Voice of America series called "In This I Believe," she referred to that day again. " 'I remember the delirious excitement I felt. And at the height of my delight, a sadness came over me, and I understood suddenly that I should not always be a child, and that beyond this carefree moment life was waiting with its responsibilities.' " [41]

The Yearling, born of that conception, describes in its first chapter Jody's intoxication with his own April moment, which extends throughout the day. It recapitulates brilliantly Mrs. Rawlings' own experience of enchantment, when she too had tasted a liquor never brewed and had become (like her Jody) dizzy and addled:

He was addled with April. He was dizzy with Spring. He was as drunk as Lem Forrester on a Saturday night. His head was swimming with the strong brew made up of the sun and the air and the thin gray rain. The flutter-mill had made him drunk, and the doe's coming, and his father's hiding his absence, and his mother's making him a pone and laughing at him. He was stabbed with the candle-light inside the safe comfort of the cabin; with the moonlight around it. He pictured old Slewfoot, the great black outlaw bear with one toe missing, rearing up in his winter bed and tasting the soft air and smelling the moonlight, as he, Jody, smelled and tasted them. He went to bed in a fever and could not sleep. A mark was on him from the day's delight, so that all his life, when April was a thin green and the flavor of rain was on his tongue, an old wound would throb and a nostalgia would fill him for something he could not quite remember. A whip-poor-will called across the bright night, and suddenly he was asleep. (14–15)

The Baxters live in a picturesque little clearing, a "pine island," in the forbidding wilderness of the ageless scrub, near Lake George and also in the vicinity of the St. Johns and Oklawaha rivers. The story covers a year's time, from April to April (1870–1871), in the course of which twelve-year-old Jody Baxter undergoes a painful series of trials, as though he must be tested for the privileges and burdens of young manhood.

Life is precarious: "Ol' Starvation" and "Ol' Death" are always at hand to threaten the Baxters and ravage their stock and their crops. Life is lonely: Ma Baxter is an old grump and there are practically never any accessible companions outside the small family, except for a little crippled boy named Fodder-wing Forrester who lives four miles away through the scrub. But there are certain compensations for all the hardships and privation. There is the big limestone sinkhole not far from the Baxter cabin and Jody often goes there to dream away an idle hour. Penny is an ideal father, a perfect mixture of the rough and the gentle, the down-to-earth and the saintly. Hunting with him is a source of unspeakable delight for Jody. And, after a long period of yearning in vain for an animal that he would be allowed to keep as a pet, Jody is given a little fawn, and his life takes on new meaning. Repeatedly the author describes the fawn, which is named Flag, as a member of the Baxter family.

Some of the other highlights of Jody's *annus mirabilis* include: his father's brush with death through a rattlesnake bite; an almost disastrous week-long rainstorm; the death of little Fodderwing; the Baxters' fight with the wild Forrester family; Penny's killing of their arch enemy, a predatory bear named Slewfoot; and Jody's disillusionment with a family friend, a sailor named Oliver Hutto. (This last circumstance, involving a preadolescent who becomes angry and baffled when his hero neglects him for some supposedly worthless woman, calls to mind Sherwood Anderson's "I Want to Know Why.")

Matters come to a head at the end of March when Flag, who is now a yearling, destroys the Baxters' future corn crop. Penny and Ora Baxter realize that whatever they plant will not be safe from the irrepressible young deer, and they conclude that he must be destroyed in order for the family to survive. Ora shoots him but only wounds him; and, since Penny is confined to bed with a serious rupture, Jody has to finish the intolerable job. Agonizing as it is for him, he somehow manages it. Then, cursing his bedridden father, he runs away from home—only to return sheepishly a few days later. And, he makes his peace with his father in the realization that he would have to go on (in the stoic tradition—described in Bigelow's book—that Penny has exemplified) without his cherished fawn.

If it were only a string of closely connected anecdotes about a young boy, *The Yearling* would be interesting and appealing enough, with its likable rascal Jody, who loves to go woolgathering, hates girls and household chores, is devoted to his noble-spirited father, and learns the harsh lessons of survival in the wilderness. But the story had been building up too long in Mrs. Rawlings' imagination and had drawn on too many of her deepest feelings for her to have produced a mere "boy's book." Throughout *The Yearling* we are reminded that man is a lost soul here on earth, at the mercy of inscrutable, whimsical forces. Penny, in his funeral sermon at the grave of Fodder-wing, addresses God: "'Hit ain't for us ignorant mortals to say what's right and what's wrong. Was ary one of us to be a-doin' of it, we'd not of brung this pore boy into the world a cripple, and his mind teched'" (211). Jody, in his flight from home after Flag has been killed, paddles down a creek in a leaky dugout and heads for the treacherous open waters of Lake George. Nature and his own mood are at one: having lost both Flag and (as it seems) his father, he is swept by loneliness. "He was out in the world, and it seemed to him that he was alien here, and alone, and that he was being carried away into a void" (416).

Mrs. Rawlings describes a nightmare world where things continue to go wrong, and where the noblest resolve, the loftiest intention, and the most arduous toil are quite unavailing. Again and again, for all the surface sentimentality that has misled serious readers, the story echoes a frightened and lost child crying in the night, out of fear, disappointment, and despair. Since there is so much in the novel that reflects the author's own life, and since this somewhat existentialist situation is seen largely through the Baxters, it is best to examine her dark, brooding drama through an analysis of the three protagonists—Ma Baxter, her husband Penny, and their son Jody.

Ma Baxter is a bitter, complaining woman who has little patience with anyone. From a casual reading of the book, she seems merely to be a dramatic foil for her husband Penny, whose deep and abiding love for his only child gives the story much of its beauty. Jody grows up father- and male-oriented, and his mother is a kind of stereotyped female ogre like the widows and aunts in *Tom Sawyer* and *Huckleberry Finn*: *She just won't let a boy have no fun nohow.* Most of the time, she gives Jody (and Penny too) "the miseries," and so the reader is tempted to write her off as a sorry example of a mother and wife. What natural boy wouldn't want to light out for the Territory?

Like a number of Mrs. Rawlings' other female protagonists, Ma Baxter suggests the author in countless significant ways. A pioneer type, she prefers the lonely wilderness with its bare minimum of social contacts; and she is fully competent to cook and "make do" under what we would consider very primitive conditions. Although she is a poor shot, like the author herself, her fierce self-reliance finds a natural outlet in the Florida backwoods, as was the case with Mrs. Rawlings from the late 1920s—when she bought her orange grove near Cross Creek—until almost the end of her life.

Penny, for all his saintliness, is too soft for Ora Baxter, who is described as being about twice his size. His relationship with his wife is typical in certain respects of what one finds in many of Mrs. Rawlings' stories: the husband in some very important way disappoints or crosses his wife, and she reacts angrily and with deep bitterness. How much of this fictional material was autobiographical is open to conjecture. Mrs. Rawlings' first marriage—to writer Charles Rawlings—ended in divorce in 1933. At the time she wrote *The Yearling* she had not yet married her second husband, Norton Baskin. (There is a very nasty dismissal of a self-consciously "professional" husband who is impossible to live with, in her *New Yorker* story of January 6, 1940, "The Pelican's Shadow.") But, just as we find Thomas Hardy's lifelong bugaboo—the "Poor Man and the Lady"—appearing again and again in his writings, the relationship between Penny and Ora Baxter, a *small* man and a *big* woman, is fairly emblematic. However, Ora's difficulties come not so much from Penny *directly* as from an actual source in the story itself.

When Penny and Jody return from the funeral of Fodder-wing, Penny tells his wife that he had never seen a family take something so hard. She snaps back, "'Don't tell me them big rough somebodies took on,'" referring primarily to the six coarse and hulking Forrester "boys," whom she cannot abide. When Penny admonishes her gently that the day may come when she will know the human heart is always the same, that sorrow strikes all over, that apparently the only thing it has done to her has been to sharpen her tongue, she replies: "'Seems like bein' hard is the only way I kin stand it.'" Then Penny goes over and strokes her hair. "'I know. Jest be a leetle mite easy on t'other feller'" (213). Ora Baxter, for all her fierce energy, has been depleted by the early deaths of numerous children. Having anticipated a large family, she was forced to watch each pregnancy end in sorrow.

The thoughtful reader may discern a mirror-image contrast between the Baxters and their distant neighbors the Forresters. Fodder-wing, a saintly child who loved all the little animals of the scrub, was the seventh Forrester son and the only one too frail to survive. Jody Baxter, the last of the seven or so Baxter offspring, was the only one hardy enough to survive. But time, man's deadliest enemy (see Mrs. Rawlings' "Cocks Must Crow"), has passed Ora by. "Jody's mother had accepted her youngest with something of detachment, as though she had given all she had of love and care and interest to those others" (20). (Robert Browning's words seem particularly applicable here: "Never the time and the place and the loved one all together.")

And Mrs. Rawlings' own deep feelings must have played some part in the shaping of Ma Baxter. It is not hard to understand why she was so unpleasant and formidable a person, or why she infused gloom and unhappiness into Jody's thirteenth year, just when the world was opening up to him. Like the author, she had been deprived, for a long time, of the opportunity for maternal expression. Even after Ma Baxter's great need had somehow been satisfied to an extent, force of habit (or an emotional lag—what I am tempted to call "emotional hysteresis") made her continue to project the customary baleful influence on those around her. It was almost as though she were lost between two worlds: the realm of *should have been* and the realm of *came too late.* Thus, in the light of the clearly developed picture we have of Jody's mother, the curt remark by the author—"Her good nature rose and fell with the food supply" (98)—cannot possibly be taken at face value. But the haunting aftereffects of a lost family constitute only part of the nightmare story that comprises *The Yearling.*

Jody Baxter's father, one of the most memorable characters in Mrs. Rawlings' writings, is a fictional realization, in a way, of her own beloved father, who was an employee in the United States Patent Office and who also owned a farm in Maryland. From him, she derived much of her deep attachment to the land and her sensitivity to the processes of nature; therefore, when she described the character of the hard-working and noble-spirited Penny Baxter, she had a perfect model from which to draw. But Penny is a man who has been severely injured by life—aside from the deaths of all the Baxter children who preceded Jody, his difficulties with his wife, and the snake-bite and the rupture that lay him low in the course of the story. His childhood, in a large farm family living near a village some distance from the Big Scrub, was characterized by adverse conditions: unremitting toil, short rations, and hookworm. His own father had been an austere preacher, and Penny's social growth was as severely stunted as his physical development. From this derived his trauma, which Mrs. Rawlings comments on vaguely but provocatively.

Why did this large-souled little man, who always wanted only what was properly his and would never kill wild game unless it was absolutely necessary, move into the primitive scrub country that was "populous with bears and wolves and panthers"? Because, the author explains mysteriously, wherever "neighbors were not too far apart, men's minds and actions and property overlapped. There were intrusions on the individual spirit." Despite all the social benefits of the settlements, there were also "bickerings and watchfulness, one man suspicious of another." Stern as his father's world had been, the world of men that Penny had grown into was "less direct, less honest, in its harshness, and therefore more disturbing." Then the author adds, as though making the ultimate revelation, "He had perhaps been bruised too often. The peace of the vast aloof scrub had drawn him with the beneficence of its silence. Something in him was raw and tender. The touch of men was hurtful upon it, but the touch of the pines was healing." However wild the animals, they "seemed less predatory to him than people he had known." The forays upon the stock of these beasts of prey he could understand, but not "human cruelties" (18).

When Jody asks his father why he moved here, " 'I jest craved peace, was all,' " he replies. " 'Out here I got it, excusin' the bears and panthers and wolves and wild-cats—and now and agin, your Ma' " (83). Enlarging upon the subject of wild-animal nature, Penny tells Jody that any mere animal can be tamed. " 'You kin tame arything, son, excusin' the human tongue' " (85). And, when Jody, thinking of Penny's deep quarrel with Lem Forrester, asks him if fights can be prevented by the curbing of fighting words, Penny thinks not: " 'I oncet seed a pair o' deef dummies havin' it. But they do say they got a sign language, and likely one passed the insult in a sign' " (187).

Like the author, Penny could not stand the press of people around him or even near him.[42] He remarks, ironically, during a deer hunt, " 'When you ain't lookin' for deer . . . they're all over the place. When you hunt 'em, you'd think you was in a tormented city' " (316). Earlier, after a disastrous rainstorm and flood, he makes a wry comment about Buck Forrester's disparagement of Doc Wilson's dark, cloistral dwellingplace in the woods: " 'If

ever'body loved the same place, we'd be right over-crowded'"
(243). Then, objecting for a moment to the Forresters' desire to
kill some of the surviving game animals, Penny says: "'Hit's a
pity we should add to their troubles. Seems like there'd ought
to be room enough in the world for folks and creeturs, both'"
(245).

What lies behind this morbid sensitivity to social encroach-
ment on the part of Penny, of Mrs. Rawlings, of many of her
fictional characters? Was it merely a kind of paranoia, finding its
expression in a solitary existence supported by a philosophy of
geographical primitivism? Actually, we are dealing with a peculiar physiological response, one not yet well understood. An
anthropologist, Edward T. Hall, who has recently begun to
explore the bio-social implications of population density, of
lebensraum, published a book on the subject, *The Hidden Dimension* (1966). In this preliminary work, he refers to the new
area of study, "proxemics," as "the interrelated observations and
theories of man's use of space as a specialized elaboration of
culture." [43] But, given our present state of knowledge, it is enough
for our purposes merely to think that a deeper explanation exists
for Penny's attitude (and the author's) than simple touchiness
or cantankerousness.

The novel derives a part of its beauty, in fact, from Mrs. Rawlings' sensitive treatment of Penny's lifelong burden which has
to do with the "bad vibrations" he has gotten and will continue to
get from other humans. (At least two ladies, playing minor roles
in the story, have a cheering rather than a grating effect on him,
and they are old friends from way back: Grandma Hutto, and
his old sweetheart, Nellie Ginright.) And Penny's basis for dealing with this burden, his hard-shelled stoicism, is the most valuable gift he is able to give to Jody. As he tells his errant, erring
son at the end of the book: "'You've seed how things goes in the
world o' men. You've knowed men to be low-down and mean. . . .
Life knocks a man down and he gits up and it knocks him down
agin. I've been uneasy all my life. . . . But ever' man's lonesome.
What's he to do then? What's he to do when he gits knocked
down? Why, take it for his share and go on'" (426).

Lastly, there is twelve-year-old Jody, growing up in isolation
and molded by his father's morbid hypersensitivity to overcrowd-
ing and his mother's pervasive and bitter pessimism. But Jody

emerges at the beginning of the story not as a neurotic, anti-social, emotional cripple, but as a wholesome country boy who is enormously excited by the renewed promise and glory of a North Florida April. The sensitive reader of any age and background cannot help but share Jody's delight in his woolgathering rambles and hunting and fishing trips, his worry over the calamities that befall his father, his fear over the threats to his family's food supply, and, finally, his ordeal in having to kill Flag, which had become a part of him and in effect a member of the family. Mrs. Rawlings' narrative is all the more effective for its directness and its lack of a programmatic mystique. A comparison, for example, of the ritual and ceremonial of Faulkner's bear-kill (in his novelette *The Bear*) with the simple bear-kill here, in which old Slewfoot is finally brought down, reminds us of the old-fashioned virtues of an uncomplicated, nonintellectualized hunt—which is not to plead for a return to ignorance or reflex activity, but merely to indicate that something is lost when the noise of the head drowns out the cry of the heart.

The alienation, confusion, anxiety, and time-sensitivity that underlie the novel are most sharply focused at the end with Jody's killing of Flag. Why should life have to be this way? Well, it just is. Jody did not believe he would ever love anybody again as he had loved Flag. "He would be lonely all his life. But a man took it for his share and went on" (427–28).

Did this climactic event in Jody's *annus mirabilis* come from the author's own inspired imagination? Bigelow, in his elaborate discussion of sources and background for *The Yearling*, traces it, and the fawn itself, to the Long family. "The idea for the pet fawn came . . . from Cal Long, whose brother Mel had had such a pet when they were boys living at Pat's Island." A considerable amount of deer lore was obtained from other sources, but "most of the details of the fawn's behavior as a pet in the home, such as his ability to open the shoe-string latch and come in at any time, she had from Cal Long, and from the same source came the climactic pathos in Jody's love for his pet, the necessity for its being destroyed because as it grew it leaped the highest fences and ate the young crops—this was also a true part of the original story of the pet deer in the Long family." [44] But there is another interesting sidelight on Jody's terrible predicament at the end.

Sometime before *The Yearling* came off the press, there appeared another masterfully narrated story about a country boy named Jody and his pet. This work (divided into a number of parts, and with a complicated publishing history) was also written in a simple, direct, emotionally appealing manner—although there is no question of literary influence on *The Yearling* by John Steinbeck's novelette. The setting for *The Red Pony* was the Salinas Valley of California, and the boy-hero, Jody Tiflin, was only ten years old; but he was also an only child, lonely and solitary, very much in need of a pet to fill the emotional void that resulted from his home life. A thumbnail summary of *The Red Pony*, taken from an old handbook on contemporary literature, somehow conveys in a flash just what it is that connects these two literary classics: "Jody Tiflin, a boy on a California ranch, is given a pony which becomes the focus of his entire life. When the pony dies he is inconsolable, even fiercely hostile toward the universe capable of such a cruelty. Later he is present at the birth of the colt which is to replace the dead pony, and he perceives the meaning of the rhythm of all living things." [45]

Another Steinbeck story is also highly significant here: the 1937 novel *Of Mice and Men*, which deals with the inflated and then exploded hopes of two close companions, migratory farm workers—George and Lennie—who are trying to save enough money for a little farm of their own. The slow-witted and child-like Lennie (who is a brute of a man) accidentally kills the young wife of the boss's son; and George (the average, ordinary man) feels obliged to shoot Lennie before the "posse" has a chance to kill him. Lennie, like Jody's fawn, has been a part of the other, normative figure; but (so runs the logic of Steinbeck's tale) he must be killed by the one closest to him if life is to go on as before. Would Jody Baxter be lonely all of his life? Must he simply take it for his share and go on? Just so is it with George, after he has killed his own alter ego (the Id part of his nature), Lennie. The civilized Ego conquers that within it which is most primitive and uncivilized.

However, there is in *The Yearling* a series of intimations culminating in a strong final statement—*not* of stoic resignation toward the blighted world men are forced to live in (Penny's scrub had proven no more satisfactory than the "world of men" he had fled)—but of belief in a shadowy and sealed off parallel

existence. Mrs. Rawlings' other novels, which end tragically or
pathetically with the death of a relative, also suggest something
of the sort, a very qualified existential solution to the spirit-
breaking problem of life's bereavement pain. Was this her own
answer to the dark forces that continued to hold her in their
grip? At the end of The Yearling Jody, drifting off to sleep
("You could call it sleep," as Henry Roth did, at the end of his
1934 novel—of that title—about a small boy's ordeal), cries out
for his lost fawn—not with his own voice but with a little boy's
voice. "Somewhere beyond the sink-hole, past the magnolia, under
the live oaks, a boy and a yearling ran side by side, and were
gone forever" (428). Is this not actually the worst part of Jody's
trial-by-fire initiation into young manhood: determining which
is the sleep, the dream—and which is the waking, the quickening
to tragic life?

III The Yearling: Novel into Film

At the time The Yearling was being launched by its publisher
early in 1938, an effort was made to sell the book to the movies;
and in April of that year Mrs. Rawlings' literary agent, Carl
Brandt, succeeded in placing the book with Metro-Goldwyn-
Mayer, which paid the author thirty thousand dollars for the
screen rights. Two years later they felt ready, for some reason,
to film the movie; and they assigned some of their biggest names
to key positions in the massive undertaking: Spencer Tracy would
play Penny Baxter, Marc Connelly (of Green Pastures fame)
would do the script, and Victor Fleming would direct.[46]

But filming a story with the kind of locale found in The Yearling proved to be vastly more difficult than was the case with
some of Metro-Goldwyn-Mayer's and the other studios' far more
exotic screenplays. Reading about the various physical discom-
forts of the Baxter family's environment (many of the discom-
forts they must have endured are not even mentioned) was one
thing. Living in that environment for the time it took to complete
a commercial motion picture of The Yearling was something else
again.

Spencer Tracy, for example, would not stand some of the
ordinary, everyday things that Mrs. Rawlings was able to put
up with philosophically for more than two decades: the red

bugs, the snakes, the heat (see chapters 14 and 15 of *Cross Creek*). There were other serious problems. The boy who was to play Jody—Gene Eckman—chose that particular time for one of his youthful growth spurts and had soon grown too big for Jody's role. When the studio executives were not able to cope with these obstacles, which were due largely to poor planning and inadequate preparation, the filming project was delayed again.[47]

In 1945 work on *The Yearling* was resumed, and Clarence Brown was assigned the job of directing the production. Prudently, he sought to use whatever he could of the aborted film project's materials and properties. A number of the animals obtained for the 1940 filming had been brought to the West Coast from Florida, and these were still available to him to take back to their Florida habitat. So, a group of animal experts including the well-known dog trainer Mack Weatherwax led a contingent of about sixty of these animals (ensconced in freight cars) to Silver Springs, Florida. Silver Springs is not far from the town of Ocala (in Marion County), which lies south of Mrs. Rawlings' old home base at Cross Creek in Alachua County, and here the beasts were settled in a two-acre zoo.

Gregory Peck had been selected for the role of Penny Baxter, and Jane Wyman for the role of Ora Baxter. An ironic commentary is hardly needed. Tall, gangly Gregory Peck to represent Jody's puny, runty father, whose character is inextricable from his small size! And Jane Wyman as the bitter, tempestuous mother? But as yet there was no one to play Jody's role; finding the "right" boy would have to wait. For the present Director Brown had to deal with the matter of locations.

The original company that Metro-Goldwyn-Mayer had created and delegated to film *The Yearling* had obtained a number of locations for the shooting of particular scenes. Some of these were now found to be quite suitable, but the single most important one—the site for the Baxter family home—was not among them. Weeks went by while Brown searched and, at last, thanks to the aid of an airplane, he found just what he wanted. He then obtained, without too much difficulty, his "genuine Cracker cabin" by requesting permission to use one that Mrs. Rawlings herself had occupied during a certain period of the composition of *The Yearling*.

The distance separating the cabin from the shooting site was not much of an obstacle. Brown had, after all, the services of a sizable labor crew at his disposal; and, with something like fifty of his men to handle the physical part of the task, he was able to transport the cabin piecemeal to its new location. Yet there was still much for his work force to do: projects such as the construction of a road, four miles in length, connecting the shooting site with the main highway, and the digging of a well, eighty feet deep, to provide the water for the necessary new plantings: corn, sugar cane, tobacco, cowpeas. While the crew on location took care of immediate practical matters, talent scouts were moving all through the South in search of a little boy who spoke like Jody would (at least, with a Southern accent), who would be photogenic, and who, of course, liked to be around animals.

But time was of the greatest importance to Brown. The story, for very good reasons, spanned a little over one year's time: from a nature-newly-risen April, through the yearling deer's death in March, and into the following April and nature's tragically sweet renewal. Thus it was necessary for Brown to set up a timetable for the actual shooting of the film script. He wanted a newborn fawn to appear in the first scenes of the movie; needless to say, the scenario would not be all that faithful to the book: Jody doesn't get his fawn until the month of June, when the novel is more than one-third along. Since does bear their young only in the spring, these first scenes would have to be shot then. Since the script called for fawns at a number of different growth stages, Brown kept a herd of deer; and he arranged somehow for the does to give birth at the desired intervals.

Thus he was able to handle the difficult matter of generative verisimilitude as far as the book's most important animals were concerned, whatever wild freedoms might be taken with the emphasis and story-line distribution of the original text. A movie miracle of time-tampering? There was also the matter of crop-growth scheduling.

Let the reader recall the importance of crop growth and maturation throughout the story, particularly near the end, when Jody's yearling insists on devouring the new shoots. Brown, following the exigencies of the script and the progress of the filmshooting, might require a young cornfield early on a particular day, and a full-grown one much later in the day. Would inexorable nature thwart his all-too-human desires? No, he would not permit it to. His workers planted corn for him, in five thousand separate cans, and at appropriate time intervals, so that a simple process of transplantation of the growing corn plants would give him what he wanted, when he wanted it. But what of the growing boy, around whom the entire picture was to be developed?

By March, and with no "Jody" in sight, Brown and his co-workers were really on the spot. Either they found someone soon, or the filming would have to be postponed until the following year, which would be very undesirable from any number of points of view. Nature and Mrs. Rawlings' story could only be circumvented so far and so long. Determined to do what he could to assist in the search, the director himself began looking all over, and he did not hesitate to call upon his Hollywood ingenuity in the emergency. Surely in some school not so very far away there must be a young boy who would fit the role. Brown developed a plan. Working with school principals in a number of Southern school districts, he was able to get them to allow him to play the part of a building maintenance man, so that he could make his way through the various classrooms at will, where hopefully he might spot "his" Jody.

Brown's scheme proved successful. One day, while he was doing his impersonation act in Nashville, Tennessee, he found what he was looking for in a fifth-grade public school classroom. The boy was ten years old—not, like Mrs. Rawlings' young hero, twelve going on thirteen. His name was Claude Jarman, Jr., and he was the son of a railroad company accountant. Claude and his family accepted Brown's movie offer, and the boy signed a seven-year contract with Metro-Goldwyn-Mayer, on a sliding salary scale which would carry him from two hundred and fifty dollars a week to one thousand dollars. There was even a further inducement: if Claude's *Yearling* venture proved successful, the contract might be revised upward.[48] As things turned out, the finished product was a big success by Hollywood standards—by box-office returns. On the strength of his performance in *The Yearling*, Claude Jarman, Jr., was given other roles and became a widely recognized child star.

In 1946 Metro-Goldwyn-Mayer's movie version of *The Yearling* finally appeared before the movie-going public. Directed by

Clarence Brown and produced by Sidney Franklin, it starred Peck, Wyman, and Jarman in the principal roles of the three Baxters; Don Gift as Fodder-wing Forrester; Chill Wills as one of the other Forrester brothers; Jeff York as Oliver Hutto; and June Lockhart as Twink Weatherby—a girl of doubtless easy virtue, who is claimed by both Oliver Hutto and Lem Forrester.

Clearly, a movie version of *The Yearling* made under Hollywood conditions against a Florida background, with tall Gregory Peck as the pint-sized Penny Baxter and a ten-year-old boy playing twelve- or thirteen-year-old Jody, is not directed primarily at the fastidious reader of the novel. As a Technicolor production, however, which closely suggests some of the important elements of the story, it makes enjoyable viewing and in fact stands up remarkably well with the passage of time. Seeing it in a motion-picture theater in October, 1971, I felt that if taken strictly on its own terms and not as a translation of the novel it had much to offer a contemporary audience.

CHAPTER 5

Inspiration's Garland:
When the Whippoorwill

THE title of Mrs. Rawlings' memorable story collection, *When the Whippoorwill*, which appeared in 1940, is taken from the nature lore of Cross Creek. "We say at the Creek, 'When the first whippoorwill calls it is time for the corn to be in the ground' "[1] (CC, 248). Most of the tales in this rich assortment deal with the life of the poor whites—the Crackers—of North-central Florida, whom the author was able to describe with remarkable intensity of feeling and in a variety of evocative moods.

I "Cocks Must Crow"

In my opinion, the finest story in *When the Whippoorwill* is "Cocks Must Crow," which appeared originally in the November 25, 1939, issue of *The Saturday Evening Post*. A tightly organized narrative, it has unusual dramatic power and psychological impact; there is not a wasted or an inappropriate word in the entire story. Through a unique narrative signature, it deals in direct and forceful terms with one of civilized man's most difficult problems: how can a husband and wife obey the command of human nature to be true to oneself above all and at the same time follow the marriage vow to love, honor, and obey each other? The language of this first-person Cracker dialect exemplum is impeccably suited to the subject. However, the Florida backwoods setting is not all that important in the story, which has a timeless, placeless, universal quality.[2] And, in addition, the story represents American frontier humor at its funniest and best.

Mrs. Rawlings' sorcerous incantation begins in the very title, with its amphimacer rhythm: cócks mŭst crów (suggesting that other long/short/long title, *Night Must Fall*). Then the narrator of the story, the vivacious and buxom Quincey Dover, delivers a long, unforgettable exordium on the subject of time and what it does to people. This bombastic opening, which sets the mood of the narrative, represents one of the author's most deeply felt concerns and is also one of the most impressive speeches in all of her writing.

I got nothing particular against time. Time's a natural thing. Folks is a kind of accident on the face of the earth, but time was here before us. And when we've done finished messing ourselves up, and when the last man turns over to die, saying, "Now how come us to make such a loblolly of living?"—why, time'll rock right on. . . .

But now what I do hold against time is this: Time be so all-fired slick. It's slick as a otter slide. And how come me to object to that, don't be on account of you slip down it so fast, but you slip down without noticing what time's a-doing to you. That's what I object to. . . .

. . . I come so clost to losing the only man a woman like me could ever hope to get a-holt of, and a good man to boot, that I can still feel the danger whistling past me like a rattlesnake striking and just missing. And that's it. Time ain't got the decency of a rattlesnake. A rattler most times'll give warning. I almost lost my Will, and me a big fat somebody no man'd look at twicet lessen he was used to me. I almost lost him on account of I had changed and didn't know it, and time never give me the first sign to warn me. Merciful jay bird! No, sir, time's a low-down, sneaking, cottonmouth moccasin, drops its fangs without you knowing it's even in the grass, and was there ary thing I could do about it, I'd do it. Excusing that, I got nothing against time. (251–52)

Quincey is a familiar female figure in Mrs. Rawlings' work: the big, assertive, sometimes cantankerous woman who is full of her own private fears and foibles. As Mrs. Rawlings wrote of herself in the autobiographical *Cross Creek*, "Time frightens me, and I seek, like a lonely child, the maternal solace of timelessness . . ." [3] (243). This type of woman, we discover in reading her fiction, is likely to marry a man smaller than herself, quite possibly someone who will sadly disappoint her and thus merit her abuse. But Quincey's marriage to the runty Will Dover is presented as something special.

Will is the perfect lover, and he is described with such love and appreciation that we are made aware of the intensity of human experience which defies literary expression—even by a skilled writer working under favorable conditions. Quincey, as she herself admits, is not such a perfect wife. For one thing, Will in the early days was so easy to get along with that their wonderful two-part harmony was due mainly to his good nature. For another thing, she *once* forgot the basic principle in handling men (i.e., in the domestication of the male animal by the female) —a principle she had originally made very good use of. In a word: a *man* (as opposed to a *woman*) is made a certain way— he *must* be allowed a degree of freedom, and he also has to know that he can exercise that freedom; therefore, a woman *must never* tie him down too tightly, for doing so would mean blocking his masculinity.

As the years pass, their fortunes wax and wane, but *they* continue in a steady state of wedded bliss. (Oddly enough, considering that part of herself which Mrs. Rawlings projected into so many of her other fictional works, Quincey appears only as a wife, never as a mother or a would-be mother.) When their circumstances change from bad to good and they prosper, the thinned-out Quincey fleshes out once more; and their life together is almost indescribably happy. Then things begin to go awry for her. Will lets on he'd like to go down to the garage and watch a cockfight that the boys are putting on. Oh no, says Quincey, cockfighting is low-down, nasty, cruel, and bloody. Will gives her some funny looks, mumbles his obedience, and saunters out. About this time a widow woman comes to settle in the village. When Quincey goes calling on her with a basket of homey gifts, right off the two of them clash over a very personal issue: Quincey's not letting Will go to a cockfight. (The widow has somehow found out about this.) After a little more faulty communication, Quincey is unable to prolong her visit, and *hmphs* away.

Suddenly Will begins taking a special interest in Quincey's fine Roundhead roosters. Can he have a couple to give to a friend?, he asks. *No.* Well, a setting of the eggs to give away to a customer of his? *No* again. By and by, Quincey notices that two of the frying-size roosters aren't there any more; and all the eggs are gone from the nests. Varmints? She and Will fall into a painful discussion about the kind of varmint that would steal chickens. Finally Will puts some money down on the table.

Fine thing, when a man has to buy chickens and eggs from his own wife . . . and when they're intended for a poor deserving soul, anyway. And who may this person be? Will is mum. Well, says Mistress Dover, there'll be no more of this kind of thing. *Yes, ma'am*, agrees Will, meaning *no, siree*. So another year goes by. And a couple more times Will lets her have additional money for a setting of eggs and some roosters.

One day when Quincey goes out to the chicken house, she finds her old basket that she'd given to the Widow Tippett—and stuck on the inside is a tail feather from one of her Roundhead roosters. The shock at Will's deception (*that sorry widow . . . Will in her clutches . . . stealing from his loving wife*) prostrates Quincey. What good was all her faithfulness to Will? What good were all her hot rations? She is filled with wounded pride as well as with self-reproach.

Quincey finally controls herself and tries to find out what has been going on. Whatever it is, Will couldn't be acting more suspiciously. Come Sunday, she spies him taking a brick out of the fireplace and sneaking out all of the money they've hidden there. He goes off, and so does his wife—to the Widow Tippett's. The two women clash again, and then Mrs. Tippett explains how it really is. Will *has* been coming to her place. No, not for affection—as far as that goes, she is getting a brand-new husband of her own. Any woman foolish enough to drive her man with a short rein, especially if he acted like Will, is making a powerful mistake. Quincey starts to wake up at last. Then Mrs. Tippett, bent on convincing Quincey, hauls her off to the woods to watch a genuine cockfight.

Not wanting to be seen there, Quincey gets up in a tree and peeks out from a limb overlooking the cockpit. She notes two different kinds of men at the disgusting spectacle. One is the cold, hard fighting man with the gambler's slow, easy way of moving. The other is a little fellow, with gentle eyes. Why would such a man be there? But she herself gets caught up in the action, becoming as enthusiastic and as partisan as anyone on the ground directly below her. When it's time for the main bout, little Will Dover comes strutting into the cockpit with a big Roundhead rooster under his arm. It happens to be one of *her* best roosters, Quincey observes, that has been turned into an impressive battle-worthy gamecock. And Quincey realizes two things: the Widow

Tippett never had fooled around with her husband; she had just let him raise and train his roosters at her place. And, Will Dover was one of the second group of participants in the cockfight—the ones she wouldn't have expected to be there. So she watches the battle royal between the Dover Roundhead and a deadly look-ing Carolina Blue. When the Roundhead is laid out cold, Quincey begins to cry. Can this be the end for the Dover champion? But, in this darkest moment, when all appears to be lost, we have a sudden "reversal of intention." The Roundhead miraculously rallies and, moved by some male impulse to do rather than die, sinks his gaffs in his adversary; the Carolina Blue drops to the ground. The contest is over.

But Quincey, perched precariously on the limb of a tree, drops when the limb cracks, right into the middle of the cockpit. Physically, she is uninjured (so runs the story line); but her spirit is hurt by the realization that time has suddenly caught up with her. Full of repentance, she makes up with the Widow Tip-pett and then with Will. They have a nice happy time of it as he takes her home at once, without waiting for the fight program to be over. She was wrong, Quincey purrs; and from now on *she*'ll raise the fighting cocks for him herself. No, Will means to quit cockfighting, because it is foolish for a man to risk losing his shirt at it; then, too, some fights get pretty ugly. He's done with that now: the need within him has been taken care of. Then follows a wonderful passage of two-part harmony, with a coy little demurrer from Quincey: " 'Will,' I said, 'home's the place for such as that.' " Which leads to the perfect ending to this rollicking Cracker saga: " 'Ain't I headed for home fast as I can go?' he said, and we laughed like a pair of young uns. My Will ain't much to look at, but he's mighty good company" (275).

This story blends quite effectively the two unrelated genres of the marriage tale and the American frontier yarn. The essence of "Cocks Must Crow" is that basic ingredient of the classic mar-riage tale—for example, Chaucer's "Wife of Bath's Tale"—the issue of who is to be the boss, and the process whereby that person becomes boss. Quincey's message to all the female readers of the story is that a husband, whatever his looks or his size, is plainly meant to wear the pants in the family, and he had better be allowed to wear them: the woman who doesn't keep this fact in mind may just lose her husband someday.

But what gives "Cocks Must Crow" (please note the title carefully) its special significance is that Quincey's husband, Will
Dover, because of his small size, his spunkiness, and his com-
mitment to cockfighting, may be closely identified with one of
the most important figures in American folklore, the "gamecock
of the wilderness." Traditionally this figure, considered to be the
"most recurrent of all American symbols of pride, defiance, and
unlimited assertion of the self," [4] has been embodied in a crowing rooster, which found its way into many literary works of the
nineteenth century. Closely related to this barnyard-fowl symbol
in American folklore is the figure of the wild, bragging, fighting
backwoodsman, often identified as the "gamecock of the wilderness." Constance Rourke, in her classic study *American Humor*
(1931), describes the type well: [5] "Heels cracking, he leapt into
the air to proclaim his attributes against all comers like an
Indian preparing for warfare. As a preliminary to a fight he
neighed like a stallion or crowed like a cock. . . . Strength was
his obsession—size, scale, power: he seemed obliged to shout their
symbols as if after all he were not wholly secure in their possession. . . . Leaping, crowing, flapping his wings, he indulged in
dances resembling beast-dances among savages . . ." [6]

Mrs. Rawlings, who eliminates the human gamecock's frenzied
boasting, makes him a bantam backwoodsman obliged to steal
from his wife the fighting cocks that will certify his masculine
power. In this cautionary tale Quincey learns some important
facts about the male animal: "Seemed to me if a rooster had the
choice, he'd a heap rather grow up to fight than perish in the
cook pot" (269–70). When Will's rooster comes out second best,
and the fight seems to be lost, Will encourages him with odd
sounds, one of which resembles the clucking of a hen, "like as if he
knowed the cock'd fight better if he figured a faithful wife was
encouraging him" [7] (271).

After the Dover Roundhead delivers his victory stroke and in
effect rises from the dead to climb upon his fallen opponent, he
crows his triumph; and a strange look comes over Will's face.
Says Quincey:

> . . . It was a deep kind of a male satisfaction. And I knowed that
> without that look a man just ain't a man. And with it, why, he's cock
> of the walk, no matter how little and runty and put-upon he be. And

I knowed why Will loved a cockfight, and I knowed why all them other little gentle-looking fellers loved it. They was men didn't have no other way to be men.

A shame come over me. Times, it's life'll do that to a man. Mostly, it's his woman. And I'd done that to my Will. I'd tried to take his manhood from him, so he didn't have no way to strut but fighting a rooster. Now he'd won, and he was a man again. And I knowed that cocks must crow. (272–73)

Quincey had been denying Will's manhood all along, *before cockcrow.* At *cockcrow,* she realized the truth about his manhood, was shamed by it, and would never again be able to make such a denial. What she had deprived him of, his fighting cock— *stolen from her*—had restored.

There are many other frontier yarn features in the story besides its local-color and tall-tale qualities, inflated rhetoric and sly deception. One is an uproarious tongue-lashing contest, a Great Debate, between Quincey and the Widow Tippett. The other is an inversion of the conventional situation in the frontier yarn, whereby the Outlander intrudes on the Native's domain and the Native puts something over on him. Here, the Native—Quincey—gets too big for her own good, loses sight of her wifely obligations, and is tricked by both husband and Outlander. But all's well that ends well in this wonderful frontier tale with all its implications of Freudian psychology, biblical symbolism, and domestic comedy. Quincey can even excuse herself a little by laying the blame for her difficulties on that sneaky varmint *time,* through whose agency she almost lost her good man in two different ways.

II *"Gal Young Un"*

The best-known story in *When the Whippoorwill* is "Gal Young Un," which appeared in the June, 1932, issue of *Harper's Magazine* and also won the O. Henry Memorial Award First Prize for 1932. It concerns, in Bigelow's words, "a worthy . . . woman of good family who married a flashy, shiftless, backwoods bootlegger." [8] Weak in characterization, "Gal Young Un" is memorable for its treatment of theme—love's betrayal—and its situational atmosphere.

The "woman of good family," Mattie Syles, lives alone in a

big old house in the hammock country. She is a widow with several thousand dollars in the bank and is sufficient unto herself. A taciturn young stranger named Trax Colton, a former resident of the area who had left when the law was on his trail, enters her life abruptly, crashing suddenly "like a meteor into the flatwoods" (189). After intruding on her rudely and finding her hospitable, he discovers that she is a woman of property; and he begins making ambitious plans. Her money and house, he reasons, can be put to excellent use in a moonshining and bootlegging operation he is thinking of starting, especially if she does a good part of the work at the still. And with that proposal Trax becomes Mattie's suitor.

After Mattie has given herself to him heart and soul, property and service, she finds out from the village storekeeper that her new, often-absent husband is only using her to run his "business" and is even carrying women around with him on his auto trips. That's her own business, she snaps: " 'What else did I have he'd want anyway!' " Mattie "understood the quality of her betrayal. The injustice was clear. It was only this: Trax had taken what he had not wanted. If he had said, 'Give me the money and for the time, the house,' it would have been pleasant to give, solely because he wanted. This was the humiliation: that she had been thrown in on the deal, like an old mare traded in with a farm" (196).

"Gal Young Un" is remarkable for its striking and unforgettable picture of frontier passion, its portrayal of Southern backwoods outrage, fury, sexual exploitation, and injured pride—as was intimated earlier. The voluptuous, stupid young sex kitten, the ill-used and physically unappealing wife, the swaggering young scoundrel, the Day of Judgment: Mrs. Rawlings mixes all of these familiar elements together, but not for purposes of sensationalism or pornography. Instead, she renders a low-keyed, sympathetic account of a strong-willed but love-starved woman eking out an isolated existence in the Florida hammock, a woman whose strength of character is put to the severest test by the man to whom she sacrifices herself.

At the core of the story is Mattie's ultimate humiliation. Trax, on a return trip home—after things have gotten too hot for him on the east coast of Florida—brings back his current mistress; and he expects his wife to put her up and let him cohabit with her. This situation is worthy of William Faulkner or Erskine Caldwell, but there is profound sadness rather than the slightest degree of prurience in Mattie's plight. Although she begins her relationship with Trax as a "loathsome hag" figure who can at least offer him material goods and personal attendance to compensate for her undesirability as a bed partner, she becomes a never-to-be-rewarded "patient Griselda," who not only gives her all to an often-absent husband but must endure continuous humiliation at his hands. And the agent of her final degradation is only a scrawny, frightened, immature "gal young un."

Two things bring matters to a head. First, Mattie, who has been getting back at Trax by mistreating his Elly—not letting her finish her meals, etc.—finds that the two of them have won her pet cat away from her. Second, Trax finally abandons Elly too: "Suddenly Trax was not taking Elly with him any more. . . . Casually he left her behind with Matt in the flat-woods" (207). On his return the next weekend, "He paid no more attention to Elly than to the older woman" (209). Somewhat later, when Mattie is certain that Trax has finished with Elly, she swings into action. On the day he returns again to his two unwanted women, Mattie destroys his still, his stores of liquor, and his expensive sedan—which she had helped finance. Then she chases the stunned and horrified Trax away from her house forever and orders Elly away too. And Mattie becomes restored as a person: "She was strong and whole. She was fixed, deep-rooted as the pine trees. They leaned a little, bent by an ancient storm. Nothing more could move them" (214).

But the ending of the story is a real capping of the climax. When Elly has no place to go and no will to get moving, Mattie now sees her in an entirely new light. Like Mattie, she is Trax's discard; so Mattie calls her back and prepares to make her a part of the household. The story ends as this odd couple arrangement is brought into being. Grotesque as their relationship may be, the situation emphasizes a curious fact: Trax has in effect given Mattie a child. Having been a widow for fifteen years and childless, Mattie felt not only affection for Trax when he came calling, but a maternal impulse as well, when he became her husband. Seeing the bridegroom in bed, Mattie "wanted to gather him up, sleeping, in her strong arms and hold him against her capacious breast" (188). But obviously she could not direct her maternal feelings to a man so predatory, nor as time went by could Mattie even retain the affection of her pet cat, on whom she had been forced to depend.

Elly, her successful rival with Trax, turns out to be the one remaining love-object for her maternal instincts. Her hatred and contempt for Trax have caused Mattie to adopt the "gal young un," to become a kind of mother to her. Elly has really been like a child, after all. Realizing what the no-account Trax has done to the "little" girl, Mattie becomes enraged. Yet she is guilt-stricken too for having condoned Trax's licentiousness, and concedes that she and Trax both should have been "hided." But, the story makes clear, at least their blighted union has not been entirely unfruitful.

III   *"Jacob's Ladder"*

"Jacob's Ladder," which appeared in the April, 1931, issue of *Scribner's,* was Mrs. Rawlings' second published story as a would-be professional writer. Bigelow, in *Frontier Eden,* calls "Jacob's Ladder," "a virtual travelogue of north central Florida, following the movements of a young cracker couple, Mart and Florry, from the flat piney woods of Dixie County above the Suwannee River, to Orange Lake in Alachua County, to the mouth of a tidal river on the Gulf of Mexico (probably the Withlacoochee), to the Big Scrub, and finally back to Dixie County." [9] The characters of Mart and Florry are based on a young couple that Mrs. Rawlings had known in her early days at Cross Creek and that are described in *Cross Creek* in the chapter "Antses in Tim's Breakfast."

"Antses in Tim's Breakfast" is only four pages long, but it contains a very important slice of Creek life as Mrs. Rawlings experienced it. The chapter opens with her declaration that most of her stories have a factual background while most of her characters combine the "true" with the "imagined." Although she cannot quite separate the two, "I do remember first a place and then a woman, that stabbed me to the core, so that I shall never get over the wound of them." Not long after arriving at Cross Creek she had discovered on the road to the village a large live oak tree, beneath which either children had been playing or someone had been living, to judge from the broken-down pieces of furniture remaining there. Later she was told that a very young man and woman had lived there during a portion of some previous summer, "coming from none knew where, and going away again with sacks over their shoulders when the autumn frosts came in." She wondered what kind of strange, fugitive people these might be.

The answer lay in her own backyard in an old decrepit tenant house beneath a large magnolia tree. Living in this collapsing hovel were that same couple and their baby. The man, Tim, was "red-haired and on the defensive and uninterested in his work. His job with the previous owner of the grove had been his first of the kind, he said. His weekly wage was low but I did not question it. He had come with the place. His passion was for trapping . . ." (64–65). But, as Tim later told Mrs. Rawlings, he was not made for grove work. " 'I don't do it to suit and it don't suit me.' " He and his family were going to live in the woods; they would do better without a house. " 'Us'll make out.' "

After they were gone, Mrs. Rawlings found that they had left a mark on her. The "small tawny lovely woman" tormented her in her dreams. "As I came to know her kind, in the scrub, the hammock and the piney-woods, I knew that it was a woman much like her who had made a home under the live oak. The only way I could shake free of her was to write of her, and she was Florry in *Jacob's Ladder*. She still clung to me and she was Allie in *Golden Apples*. Now I know that she will haunt me as long as I live, and all the writing in the world will not put away the memory of her face and the sound of her voice" (67–68).

"Jacob's Ladder" opens with a scene that suggests a North Florida version of a Thomas Hardy setting: rural, preindustrial Dorset; a country dance; a rustic fiddler; and everybody's favorite old-time tunes. At a square dance in a cabin in the pine-woods, one of the local characters, an aging widower named Jo Leddy, is happily drunk; and an argument breaks out between his former lady friend and his current sweetheart. Then his rabbity little daughter—his only child, apparently in her teens—enters and is brusquely ordered to leave by her boisterous father. She sits on the cabin stoop and is joined by a young Cracker boy of about her age, who is also ragged, gaunt, and rabbity. They exchange a few words. Then a whippoorwill calls "uncertainly" to his mate. "Suddenly the girl knew that this man was not a stranger. He was like herself. More, he was a part of herself. She was a part of him. It was altogether natural that they should be sitting together" this way (46–47).

The pastoral, Hardyan opening of this lugubrious tale is especially significant. Two Cracker strays are drawn together by some mystic, elective-affinity bond. There is little joy in their encounter—both are afflicted by poverty, ignorance, and the general wretchedness of an uncertain existence. The next day the boy makes his way to the Leddy cabin, six miles away in a little clearing in the woods, to claim his mate. It happens that a fierce Florida gale is raging—the terms *gale* and *hurricane* are used interchangeably in this story—and Mart, the boy, arrives during a lull. When he asks Florry to go off with him, she is ready, having sensed this would happen, just as she had sensed the coming of the gale. Her violent-tempered father, who would surely oppose her leaving, is in a drunken stupor, and so there is nothing to hinder them. She and Mart go out into the harsh storm to make a life together. Only a piece of paper on which a Yankee had once written her name remains as a token of her existence.

From this point on the story is one long succession of miseries, hardships, heartbreaks, and betrayals, as the luckless and slow-witted Mart tries working on a citrus grove, trapping, saltwater fishing on the Gulf of Mexico, and moonshining. Given the circumstances of their little baby's death, their incessant grinding poverty, the treachery of trusted associates, and Mart's thirty-day stretch on the road gang—for moonshining—"Jacob's Ladder" is somewhat reminiscent of a nineteenth-century Russian tragedy. As each new adversity forces them to pick up stakes and seek a living elsewhere, Florry to her sorrow must forsake some little creature she has come to love. "She had minded leaving old Sport behind, and the cat and the 'coon, and butchering the pig for rations. She minded the puny baby lying on a Yankee's land, under a Yankee woman's petunias. It came to her that if Mart had stayed on the clearing, in old Jo's cabin that she had a right to, she would still have the hound, and it might be the baby. They had let their fear move them on" (101).

The theme of the story is found in the title, which has to do with the old spiritual Florry hums about the ladder from earth to heaven that was seen by Jacob in a dream (Genesis 28:12). The refrain "When I lay my burden down!" has relevance to

Florry's personal burden of saving and preserving herself under extremely adverse conditions. Before going away with Mart, she had had to endure her father's mistreatment and hostility; but *her own courage* had sustained her when there was no other source of help. Once she took up with Mart, this was no longer necessary: "She had laid her burden down on his lean, strong knees" (109). But, toward the end of the story, when the last blow strikes Mart—the loss of his traps (on which he was totally dependent for sustenance) to a dishonest storekeeper in cahoots with a dishonest sheriff—Florry undergoes a striking change. She thinks, " 'I've done had me a rest, like.' A burden laid down could be picked up again" (109). Her mainstay, Mart, is frightened and demoralized, unable to function: " 'There ain't nothin' left to try. There ain't no'eres left to go. We been a-climbin' ol' Jacob's ladder thouten no end to it' " (110).

But Florry has taken over. It doesn't matter what happens to them now, she insists. They shouldn't be afraid. People are worse than storms, so they should get themselves a place where no one can harm them, a place they have a right to be in. And there is such a place: her father's cabin, which is really her dead mother's cabin, far away in the pine-woods they had left long ago. If Mart would just stand up to her father, let him have it once, maybe, to show him she has her rights too. Mart, now sick with a fever, can't see making such a trip; but, when Florry insists, they begin the long trek back.

The last portion of the story describes their agonizing journey home: "No cypress log had tugged so ponderously against her [old Jo had made her work as a logger in shoulder-high swamp water] as the burden of Mart's heavy spirit. He followed her like a hound unwilling at heel" (112). They finally reach the Leddy cabin *in the middle of a hurricane*, as if to complete the circle of their stormy life away from where Mart had found Florry. Old Jo is alone, and he greets his returned daughter by trying to crush her with a heavy piece of wood. When Mart subdues Jo and reduces him to a "frightened, old and beaten" hulk, Florry's "ancient terror" of him is gone. But the hurricane is still raging; and Mart, disgusted that the old man has never replaced the kitchen door that had blown off, finds the door, puts it back, and secures it with a pine sapling. Florry asks him if he can make it stay shut now. " 'Hit'll hold,' he said" (117–18).

"Jacob's Ladder," despite its colorless characters, leaves us with a number of strong impressions, as well as with a final message. The burden of resisting life's ravages should not be laid down by the woman. There is no telling what ultimate harm will result if she allows the load to lie fully on anyone else's shoulders, particularly her man's.

IV The Other Stories

There are eight other stories in When the Whippoorwill, but aside from "A Mother in Mannville"—discussed in chapter 4— none is particularly remarkable. Two of these remaining stories are narrated by Quincey Dover: "Benny and the Bird Dogs" (Scribner's, October, 1933) and "Varmints" (Scribner's, December, 1936). At one time, Bigelow states, Mrs. Rawlings had the idea of preparing an entire volume of stories featuring this fat Cracker heroine with the gift of gab.[10] Bigelow lumps together all three Quincey Dover tales and another comic vernacular narrative, "Alligators"—the material for which was supplied by the author's friend and neighbor, Fred Tompkins—as a portion of her work having the highest literary value, along with The Yearling and Cross Creek.[11] According to Bigelow, her "great gift for the vernacular is best seen in her comic stories, which are in the tradition of the frontier tall tale. They have the classic elements established by Mark Twain—a folk narrator speaking in the vernacular, a surface realism coupled with wild exaggeration. The characters are grotesques." [12]

The point is not whether Mrs. Rawlings is using vernacular language, but rather how significant is the story, how deeply does it affect the reader. We are dealing here with amusing but very light entertainments. "Benny and the Bird Dogs" is a series of reminiscences about old Uncle Benny Mathers, constable at Oak Bluff, who was passionately devoted to his bird dogs and was always "cutting the fool." As for how such a clownish old reprobate could be an officer of the law, "We figure it keeps him out of worse trouble to let him be constable" (21). "Varmints" is about Quincey's troubles with an unnatural mule belonging to two of her acquaintances. "Alligators," as the name implies, is a rambling series of recollections about the general orneriness of Florida 'gators. There is no spellbinding here, no "high sentence," no distinctive vocal signature. The stories are pitched at the level of low farce, laugh-grabbing buffoonery, which is too often the case with frontier tales depending on wild exaggeration. William Faulkner himself was susceptible to this kind of simple rustic comedy, and "Varmints" in fact seems to have a great deal in common with his bagatelle "Mule in the Yard."

"A Crop of Beans" (*Scribner's*, May, 1932) suggests a bitter-sweet version of "Jacob's Ladder." The narrative is alternatingly amusing and sad, as Mrs. Rawlings describes the plight of a poor Cracker field hand, Lige Gentry, who toils for a sharp-tongued, sadistic old woman, the Widow Sellers, and then tries desperately to grow his own crop of beans. Only by having his own bean crop can Lige really fulfill himself and, at the same time, properly support his family. There is a child's fairy tale quality to Lige's ups and downs with his beans, particularly the "last straw," when a local bank failure wipes out practically all he made on a re-markable bumper crop. "A Plum Clare Conscience" (*Scribner's*, December, 1931) is a whimsical, ironic tale about a moonshiner who slyly outwits, and outwaits, some revenue agents.

"The Enemy" (*The Saturday Evening Post*, January 20, 1940), which concerns Florida cattlemen and the march of progress, ironically places an old-timer, who shows disrespect for someone else's property rights and an unwillingness to accept economic realities, in the position of enemy to his own kind and his own kin. The story has a "sunny skies" ending, and an *amor vincit omnia* message. The *enemy's* son comforts his young wife and banishes her fears about the future. First the intruding Yankee cattleman had been the enemy. Then the girl's father-in-law became the enemy. Possibly the real enemy was the injurious drought. Finally she realizes that the enemy was actually life itself; and then her husband solaces her with his love. She laughs with relief. "Her love was a lean, hard bulwark against the foe" (174).

Lastly, "The Pardon" (*Scribner's*, August, 1934)—discussed in chapter 4—describes the *dream-child*, the child that wasn't supposed to be there, big as life and demanding to be dealt with. And, once more, initial rejection of destiny's waif will *apparently* be followed by a reconsideration of the matter and finally a con-strained acceptance.

Though the Cracker studies in *When the Whippoorwill* are of uneven quality, the book on the whole is fascinating, clearly the work of an accomplished writer of fiction. Unaccountably, Mrs. Rawlings' first Cracker story, "Cracker Chidlings" (*Scribner's*, February, 1931)—actually, a string of anecdotal sketches—is omitted from the collection. "Cracker Chidlings," which may be said to have inaugurated Mrs. Rawlings' literary career, is a series of eight little vignettes of Cracker life: "Real Tales from the Florida Interior" was the subtitle of the work. The eight sketches are given titles: "Squirrel Eyes"; "Even a Snake"; "A 'Shiner's Wife"; "Georgia Money"; "The Jest"; "Grampa Hicks"; "The Preacher Has His Fun"; "The Silver River."

There is nothing memorable or even provocative, today, about these pieces except that they prefigure Mrs. Rawlings' serious later work. But, taken as hints or "notes toward a definition of" Florida Cracker life, they might well have stimulated in early readers a demand for more of this colorful regional writing; indeed, the Scribners editors predicted correctly that there would be a continuing market for stories based on such raw material. Running through these "chidlings" is the idea of deeply ingrained hostility between the Florida Crackers and their counterpart to the north, the Georgia Crackers. Aside from making it evident that the two groups hate each other by virtue of their home state, Mrs. Rawlings does not explain the basis of this antagonism so that it can be appreciated by the reader. Nor in fact do her subsequent fictions really go into this matter.

However, from the various references to intruding outlanders in *South Moon Under*, the reader easily gathers that isolation and economic hardships fostered a morbid insecurity and suspiciousness on the part of the Florida Crackers (who were, essentially, poor whites). As a result of such external constraints, geographical rivalries developed; it is not entirely surprising that the Georgia Cracker should be regarded by the Florida Cracker as being little if any better than a Yankee. As to why "Cracker Chidlings" plays up this geographical-social antagonism while her later work ignores it, we must assume that the more deeply Mrs. Rawlings immersed herself in Cracker lore and folkways the less important this holdover from early frontier-settlement times became.

"Squirrel Eyes" pictures a "free feed" of squirrel pilau and Brunswick stew given by an *apparently* magnanimous Cracker for the Crackers of two counties. "Even a Snake" is an extended remark about a Cracker who returned home unexpectedly and found his friend lying in *his* bed while *his* wife was busily stirring the fire in the hearth. "Grampa Hicks" is a vignette of an old reprobate who doesn't mind doing anybody out of anything, but whose religion does not permit him to go fishing on Sunday. "The Silver River" is about another old reprobate, a kind of Kentucky Colonel, who defrauds a widow of some valuable river land and then has this land stolen from him, in turn, by a shrewd Cracker judge. (This is a rare instance in Mrs. Rawlings' writings of a Cracker rising to high or even relatively high position.) "Georgia Money" is a sketchy account of a rascally Florida Cracker's troubles with his Georgia wife.

Probably the best of these eight modest pieces is "The Jest," which should have been developed into a short story with appropriate local color and dramatic buildup. But Mrs. Rawlings merely describes a local practice of the time, a variation on the ancient folk custom of putting something over on the ignorant outlander. "The Jest" *tells* (where it should *show*) how the very occasional youth who comes to the "hamlet"—as she calls it—is victimized by the local boys: he is fooled painfully into thinking that one of them is going to procure him a girl who has been secretly yearning for him. This nasty but amusing trick involves entrapment, female impersonation, and sadistic humiliation of a single individual by a sizable group; and the incident reflects the dark, ugly side of Cracker life which is occasionally dealt with in Mrs. Rawlings' work; other instances are what might be called "vigilante justice" and the killing of a revenue agent or an informer who is seriously threatening a Cracker's moonshining operation.

However undeveloped or trivial these "Cracker Chidlings" are, they provide so effective an introduction to the major body of Mrs. Rawlings' work that a story collection such as *When the Whippoorwill* seems strikingly incomplete without them.

CHAPTER *6*

Land of Heart's Desire: *Cross Creek*

I Toward a Definition of Cross Creek

READING *Cross Creek* now, over thirty years after it was written, we are taken directly into the primitive, slow-time atmosphere of the North Florida backwoods with its lakes and rivers and hamlets that Mrs. Rawlings so closely identified herself with for more than two decades. Lochloosa Lake, Orange Lake, the River Styx, the Oklawaha River, Island Grove, Citra, Hawthorne, McIntosh constituted the prospect before her, as well as the medium through which she was able to define herself, until the time came when a geographical and spiritual recycling seemed called for. Here, in Southeastern Alachua County near the boundaries of Putnam County and Marion County, about twenty-five miles (as the crow flies) from Ocala to the south, and sixteen or so miles from Gainesville to the northwest, she established her home and her being as a writer.

Cross Creek itself, in terms of a body of water, is the narrow neck that connects Lochloosa Lake on the northeast with Orange Lake on the south. (Bigelow's *Frontier Eden* contains excellent pen-and-ink maps and sketches, on the inside covers, of this general area—Robert E. Carson is the artist.) In terms of Mrs. Rawlings' "territory," Cross Creek may be considered the immediate area east (rather, southeast) of the neck uniting the two lakes. The hamlet of Island Grove, she explained, was four miles to the east of where she lived.

Mrs. Rawlings was proud of her grove property, for a number of reasons, as *Cross Creek* makes clear. Originally it had been part of a Spanish grant from the crown to Don Fernandez de la Maza Arredonda and his son. According to tradition, which she accepted in this case, those Spanish land grants had conferred good orange-growing land on the grantees. Something in her responded to her grove's subtle challenge, and over the years she would resolutely contend with the vagaries of climate and the uncertainties of Cross Creek soil in an ongoing effort to produce bountiful crops of "golden apples" from the hammock land. (Bigelow, in *Frontier Eden* [73–74], provides a cogent summary of her experiences as a citrus grower, and touches on the recurring menace of crop freeze, which she faced directly a number of times.)

One source of this response, this answer to the "call" of the land, was her farming heritage, through the Traphagens on her mother's side and the Pearces on her father's. She was in effect returning, at least for a time, to *an* ancestral place, picking up again where her forebears had left off, and finding satisfaction in doing so. More importantly, living and working in Cross Creek, where only a small handful of white and black families made their home, gave her a sense of continuity with nature, with all living things and with the cosmos. In this feeling she found comfort when private griefs and miseries assailed her. The very paradox of the sparsely settled, out-of-the-way Cross Creek area —rich, teeming life in a biological sense; poverty of experience in a human sense—fired her imagination as it aroused her loyalties and her writing talent.

She wrote of life at Cross Creek as a fulfillment of her inmost being, in fact a finding of and remaining with the individual's (*her*) own true love. Not that all problems would thereby be eliminated, particularly the persistent problem of loneliness. Loneliness, she realized, was a human condition to be endured wherever one chose to live. However, no other dwelling place could she consider seriously, least of all an urban environment, which to her would be the worst of hells.

In trying to explain the unexplainable, that is, her affinity for the "land," Mrs. Rawlings fell back on a mystique of origins (see particularly the introduction to the book, also titled "Cross Creek") and on what she referred to as "racial memory." Had she taken a cue or derived some of her more important thoughts from Carl Jung? Our ultimate parent, she felt, was the earth (land *and* water), which has a claim on us prior to that of any human ancestors. In her view man cannot survive if he is separated from the earth, and he will not remain whole if he forsakes the earth to involve himself solely in human affairs. (By the time Mrs. Rawlings had completed her last book, *The*

Sojourner, she had changed her mind completely about our earth's being necessary for human survival.) But Mrs. Rawlings was a sensitive environmentalist, and she clearly realized that not everyone would do well in any one particular place. It was clearly a matter of suiting the individual (human or animal) to what for him was the exactly suitable background: some creatures, for example, could not stand certain changes of locale. Her own transfer to Cross Creek was, we gather, the thing she had unwittingly been waiting for all or most of her life.

Unless we first put aside our own preferences and preconceptions we will not be able to understand even vaguely how Mrs. Rawlings could give herself so intensely—not completely, by any means, and certainly not permanently, just intensely—to a particular spot in the North Florida woods. For those who fail in understanding this aspect of Mrs. Rawlings, a reading of Walker Percy's 1961 novel, *The Moviegoer* (which reveals Percy's extraordinary sensitivity to locale and to the quality of human experience in relation to a particular place), may assist them in fitting temporarily into Cross Creek. The point is that Mrs. Rawlings was transformed by this environment and that she tried her hardest, in this book and particularly in the first chapter, "For this is an enchanted land," to suggest the attractive power of the Cross Creek area.

Mrs. Rawlings attempted to convey the aura of enchantment she felt by making an association with the classic woodland tales of childhood and with the ancient Druids: the dim, mystical, forested past now somehow restored. She described the curving, four-mile-long road making its way from Island Grove to the Creek through pines and gallberries, then through a thick growth of hammock, finally revealing—in the interior of the hammock and on both sides of the road—the magical orange grove, which made her feel as if she had entered another world.

One basis for her enchantment with Cross Creek is particularly interesting. Watching the trees and plants and crops (to say nothing of the animal life) in all their stages of growth throughout the seasons of the year gave her a peculiar and somehow reassuring feeling of timelessness. *Time* was, after all, a constant enemy: she had an intense fear of time, a dread of being harmed or at least seriously endangered by it. But growing things had a natural way of getting the better of time. They decayed and died, true enough, but they came back again before long and were just as sturdy and pleasing to the human senses as ever. By feeling herself to be a link, a part of this process, she took courage and faced with serenity and optimism the sloughing off of the calendar's leaves. Some of the most effective writing in this entire book (most of which, actually, is beautifully 'rendered) deals with her perception of seasonal changes as they affected the flora and fauna of the Creek.

The memorable soliloquy at the end—dealing with the question of who really owns Cross Creek—is a fitting climax to the book. The birds own this region, she concludes; human claims are not so valid as theirs. In fact, the Creek belongs to the elements, "to the cosmic secrecy of seed, and beyond all, to time" (368). Mrs. Rawlings, like Faulkner, fell back on the ancient Anglo-Saxon idea of land*holding*, land *use*, land *loving, tending, tenancy*, rather than land *ownership*. And her soliloquy is worth memorizing and ranking with Faulkner's statements on landholding, with George Meredith's great poem, "Life is but a little holding, Lent to do a mighty labor," and with Robert Frost's poem "The Gift Outright."

II *As* Walden *was to Thoreau . . .*

Reading *Cross Creek* in the light of Mrs. Rawlings' extreme introversion, we are quickly reminded of Thoreau's *Walden* (1854) and to a lesser extent of his *A Week on the Concord and Merrimack Rivers* (1849). But *Cross Creek* and *Walden* really do not compare closely. Although each author wrote out of some deep private pain, purposing to remedy a grievous hurt and ward off a nameless but insistent danger, Mrs. Rawlings lived many years longer in her retreat than Thoreau did in his. He was the greater prose poet, and his concern was with how men ought to live. Thus, while *Walden* is directed to the reader as an *Imitatio Thoreauviani*, the other book is directed to the reader as a personal account of life in the woods, and it is not a biographical manifesto for social revolution or change. Beautiful as *Cross Creek* is, and poetically philosophical, it has nothing to compare with Thoreau's "Battle of the Ants," with his epigrams about the *individual* ("moving to the beat of a distant drum"), and the *mass of men* ("leading lives of quiet desperation");

nothing to match his reiterated threnody of loss (for example, the figurative reference to the hound, the bay horse, and the turtle-dove). And yet, as we who read it will discover, *Cross Creek* is quite able to stand on its own literary merits and appeal to a wide variety of reading tastes.

The book is a record of Mrs. Rawlings' experiences of about a thirteen-year period spent in and around Cross Creek. As the book makes clear, the affinity she felt with the region reshaped her being in a way that must appeal to the most urbanized sensibility. In a much earlier society, she might well have con-sidered changing her name to express this new self more ac-curately: *The Northern Lady Who Found a New Home in Cross Creek*, perhaps. The title of her first chapter tells the story: "For this is an enchanted land."

Because *Cross Creek* is so intensely personal, it is difficult to summarize it in any systematic fashion. Mrs. Rawlings wrote as an amateur naturalist, and her frequent detailing of flora and fauna places her firmly within a given, meaningful space, while her occasional vagueness about time gives an odd impression of existential drift. By condensing a few of the lively, revealing anecdotes that inform and illuminate the book, we may however give some indication of the personally enriching life she lived at the Creek.

One of the Creek characters, Mister Marsh Turner, was a walking contradiction, two different men confined in a single body. Outwardly a drunken, obstreperous troublemaker and general hell raiser, he was at the same time (in Mrs. Rawlings' view, at least) a peaceful man of good breeding. But he did live carelessly—letting his livestock range freely over his neigh-bors' property, for example—in an old decaying house with his elderly mother. His Saturday night drinking bouts were particu-larly disturbing. He happened also to be a lover of music, and it was nothing for him to break into some festivity and take over from the fiddler—not sticking to the tune being played, but, as we would say today, "doing his own thing." Most weekends found him in jail, but on Monday morning he would pay his fine in a friendly manner, and on arriving home get drunk again. Then the familiar pattern: falling into a rage, he would start throwing heavy objects around.

But making amends somehow was as much a part of his nature

as causing the damage in the first place. Once, when Mrs. Rawlings became fed up with what his rampaging livestock had been doing to her property, she threatened either to summon the law or to take the law into her own hands and impound his animals. He came to see her in a very intoxicated state, and with tipsy gallantry announced that any of *his* stock that bothered her in the future would then be *her* stock. There were several versions of how Mister Turner died. The version Mrs. Rawlings chose to believe was in keeping with what she had known about him. When the sheriff came to arrest him one day for causing a lot of damage in a total stranger's house, Turner held out his gun and told the sheriff that the gun was for him—whereupon the law officer shot him dead. But Marsh had not intended any challenge; he was simply giving up his weapon.

Then there was the "odd couple" situation, which began with a ménage à trois. One of the men at the Creek found a destitute couple out in the flatwoods. The wife appealed to him in some way, and he cleaned her up and then took both of them home with him. For a time, things went well. The husband would leave his much younger wife alone with his benefactor during the day while he went fishing on the lake. Finally the time came when the husband did not like this arrangement any more; he announced suddenly that either both men would fish out on the lake, or he would start staying home too. So his host agreed, and they fished together. While both men were absent from the house, something seemed to them to be amiss; each became suspicious. Then the couple moved away, the wife going in one direction and the husband in another. Not long afterward the woman became seriously ill, and the doctor made it clear that she was dying. The two men returned to help take care of the patient. After her death, both of them "went away together, and the last I heard were farming and sharing, like good bachelors, the housework" (364).

The chapter titled "My Friend Moe" tells about a kindly carpenter whom she came to know and respect. Moe paid a formal call on Mrs. Rawlings on her first Christmas day in Cross Creek, coming at an awkward time—she was preparing a huge, fancy meal for her guests—then staying for dinner but appreciating it not in the least, and finally shaming her when she irritatedly asked him what a typical Cracker Christmas dinner was like.

" 'Whatever we can git, Ma'am,' he said. 'Whatever we can git' "
(110). As they came to know each other better, each helped the
other in countless ways. On one occasion Moe gave Mrs. Rawlings
a valuable antique bed that had been in his family's possession
for many years. On another occasion, he prevented her young
Valencia orange trees from perishing in a severe freeze. A care-
burdened man with twelve children and a dull-witted, slovenly
wife, Moe appreciated Mrs. Rawlings' enterprise and her housekeeping talents.

Once she was able to do him a genuine service when his
youngest child, Mary—the only one of the family who really
cared about him—lay critically ill with pneumonia. There was no
one to help but Mrs. Rawlings, who had been preparing to leave
by train for New York for an editorial conference. Setting aside
her own urgent plans, she drove to Ocala in a heavy rainstorm
—in a farm truck with a leaky roof—procured the aid of a doctor
and nurse for Mary, and saw to it that Moe, currently penniless,
would have enough money to manage until he could get work
again. Later, when the overburdened and undernourished Moe
breathed his last, it was only Mary—the model for Doll Linden
in *The Sojourner*—who seemed to be deeply affected by his
passing. There is also a moving account of the death of Mrs.
Rawlings' old mule, Joe; she ends by talking about the different
kind of grass that grew the following spring where Joe had
walked on tether. (This passage suggests the description of the
death of the donkey in Juan Ramon Jimenez' *Platero and I*
[1956].)

In her "Fall" chapter she presents a little vignette of a couple
she once encountered briefly, old man Butler and his wife, who
lived at Orange Lake Station. The two were locked in a painful
and all but insoluble domestic dilemma—what the critics might
call a "pastoral vs. anti-pastoral" conflict. Butler was in a continual
state of intoxication from the peacefulness and the beauty (as he
saw it) of his farm and from the feeling of independence it gave
him. But his wife could not stand the isolation and the emptiness
of their farm existence. And they battled unhappily over their
likes and dislikes. Mrs. Rawlings, as we might readily surmise,
sympathized entirely with Butler. And, with curt satisfaction,
she reported what finally happened to the quarrelling Butlers
long after she had made their acquaintance. The local newspaper

carried an account of the old man's death; but he had still been living at Orange Lake Station.

In her chapter on "Summer" we find a personal anecdote that offers more food for thought than do many of the others. It concerns the proper training of a hunting dog—the discipline that must be rigidly applied if one is to obtain the desired results. Her story is particularly ironic when we consider that she was neither a good shot nor a wholehearted supporter of the animal-killing aspect of hunting. One June evening she came in contact with a dog belonging to a neighbor of hers. Walking along the Creek road, she felt lonely and uneasy (thinking of the poisonous snakes); and a mongrel dog passed her way, following a ramshackle car. Her heart went out to the poor forlorn animal, and she attracted his attention and gave him the encouragement and affection he needed so badly. They became friends, and she was happy to have the company of a dog after not having had one for so long. But, she points out in her account, a *business* (or *working*) dog, which this one was, is made differently than other dogs and does not expect lavish treatment; he has a job to do, and is grateful for the infrequent show of friendship that he may receive.

A close but very special relationship developed. In the late afternoons and evenings they romped and roamed together in idyllic harmony. On one occasion the dog even saved her from a large rattlesnake. But then, it turns out, Mrs. Rawlings received the highly bred pointer puppy she had long awaited. She had made careful plans and now was obliged to turn her attention to him, training him carefully and rigorously, since he was to be a *real* companion to her. Under these circumstances, the former dog would not only be in the way but would be a definite liability. So, now she had to reject the working dog whenever he came to play or made it his business to try to keep their friendship going. And, firmly and coldly, she succeeded over the next several days in driving the dog away and in keeping him away. The author concludes this sad account on a note of self-above-all candor. She and the dog became strangers to each other, and she could not bear facing the animal since she had made use of him in her "loneliness, and then betrayed him. He shows no signs of recognition. His tail curves over his back. He trots with a high head, looking straight ahead. He is a work dog, and he must be about his business" (297).

One of the many wryly amusing stories is given in chapter 4, "The pound party" (anthologized a number of years ago in a college English reader). It concerns the author's experiences with a shiftless but importunate family at the Creek. Recast in terms of the folktale, the story would have the grasshopper successfully parasitizing the ant, and teaching the ant how to get ahead.

It is interesting that one finds in her more outspoken social commentaries faint echoes of Thoreau, who, for all his attachment to his woods and exaltation of the human spirit, did not love his fellowman very much. We recall the irritability he felt when he was approached too closely or imposed upon in some way; the various defenses he used: standoffishness, snobbishness, disaffiliation, even contempt. He was easily wearied by human contacts. Both Thoreau and Mrs. Rawlings must have been allergic to the press of too many people, especially people who were not the *right sort*. Despite their differences in background, these two rustic naturalists, occasional poets, and isolates seem somehow oddly related. The important quality that Thoreau shared with Mrs. Rawlings is the tendency to *observe*, through one's prejudices, the passing parade. Neither writer was a genuine social reformer, however much advice the reader may find in *Walden* and in *Cross Creek* about how to live the good life. What if Thoreau once did "help to forward a real runaway slave toward the northstar." What if he claimed to "know of no more encouraging fact than the unquestionable ability of man to elevate his life by a conscious endeavor" (*Walden*, "Where I Lived, and What I Lived For"). What if he was *occasionally* gregarious, strolling every day or so to the village for the gossip "which, taken in homoeopathic doses, was really as refreshing in its way as the rustle of leaves and the peeping of frogs" (*Walden*, "The Village"). Most of the time he was content to record what he saw, take care of his own needs, and accept the social status quo, however unjust it might be. And so with Mrs. Rawlings, particularly in regard to the low position of Negroes in Florida in the 1930s.

However, even if we allow for the mores of Mrs. Rawlings' time and place, it is difficult to summarize her real feelings about

Negroes and to assess her attitude as tolerant, prejudiced, egali-
tarian, or anything else. She was sensitive to class differences
as well as to color differences, and, although a number of passages
could be cited from *Cross Creek* as evidence of a racial bias,
there were times when she reflected a larger sympathy toward
all struggling humans. We find an assortment of anecdotes and
vignettes in *Cross Creek* about domestic difficulties and irregu-
larities among the Negroes of the Creek and about the author's
Servant Problem—as far as Negroes are concerned. Unedifying
and in fact embarrassing as some of the stories are, they must
be read in the light of her deep affection and respect for individuals such as "Aunt" Martha Mickens, whom she would no
more have looked down on than William Faulkner would have
looked down on Mammy Caroline Barr, to whom he dedicated
one of his books.

Yet again, in her "Black Shadows" chapter—which is anticipated in her *Collier's* story, "In the Heart"—Mrs. Rawlings is so
painfully outspoken about the whole matter of race relations that
only the perspective of history can prevent a sensitive reader
from wincing. "I am not of the race of southerners," she begins,
"who claim to understand the Negro." Such "southerners" hold
tightly to certain platitudes about the Negro "that seem reason-
ably accurate": he is only a child; he is gay, carefree; he is
amusingly religious; he is a born liar; the best Negro cannot be
depended upon. These are "superficial truths" and behind them
"lies the mystery of the primitive African nature, subjected
precipitously first to slavery and then to so-called civilization,"
both equally difficult and unjust. "In the South his wages are a
scandal and there is no hope of racial development until racial
economics are adjusted." Until this happens, the Negro continues,
apparently, to be "childish, carefree, religious, untruthful and
unreliable" because of a very deeply ingrained defense mecha-
nism. Only in this way could he "adapt himself to the injustice of
his position and to the master white race."

There is a "prettier side of the picture . . . the possibility of
real affection between individuals of the two races," qualified
by the fact that one race is master, the other still a slave. In this
position the Negro has two different weapons: he can make his
employer's life not worth living, or he can walk off the job. If a
Southern Negro uses neither weapon, it is probably because of a

true attachment to his mistress or master. Even if he feels a true love for the latter, he may still use one of the two weapons. "Therein lies his unpredictability . . ." (180–81).

Thus, as indicated above, like that other solitary nature-observer and lofty thinker—Thoreau—Mrs. Rawlings often came down from the clouds and showed clearly by her condescension and petulance how constraining human relationships (even tenuous ones) could be. Small wonder that she would sometimes get carried away by her irritable temperament and make too-provocative remarks, as in the case of her comments on Zelma Cason, comments that led to a long-drawn-out libel suit.[1] In 1930, Zelma Cason, a friend of hers, was made census taker "in the back country sections of Alachua County" (where Cross Creek is located). Zelma, Mrs. Rawlings stated bluntly, "is an ageless spinster resembling an angry and efficient canary. . . . I cannot decide whether she should have been a man or a mother. She combines the more violent characteristics of both . . ." (48).

In her chapter on "The magnolia tree" (which ends with a hymn of praise to "the cosmic life" silently pulsing through all things) she speaks feelingly of her own "irreducible minimum of happiness": merely "a tree-top against a patch of sky" (28). In the sixth chapter, "The evolution of comfort," she describes the old outhouse near her Creek home and tells gleefully how she built first one and then a second indoor bathroom. And, once more in a mood of rollicking good humor, she develops a marvelous porcine chapter, "A pig is paid for."

One of the two most beautiful chapters in the book, "Hyacinth drift"—which appeared in its original form in the September, 1933, issue of *Scribner's*—takes her away from the Creek on a therapeutic river-journey several hundred miles down the St. Johns in an eighteen-foot, outboard-motor boat. After the journey and return, she gained a new appreciation of the Creek. One afternoon, at Welaka, she and her companion, Dessie, "left the hyacinths swirling leisurely and turned up our home river . . ." Now on the Oklawaha, she "thought in a panic, I shall never be happy on land again. I was afraid once more of all the painful circumstances of living." But, once on dry land, she "found a forgotten loveliness in all the things that have nothing to do with men." Beauty pervaded the land now: "Because I had known intimately a river, the earth pulsed under me. The Creek was home. Oleanders were sweet past bearing, and my own shabby fields, weed-tangled, were newly dear. I knew, for a moment, that the only nightmare is the masochistic human mind" (357– 58). Thoreau's Concord and Merrimack have more than a little in common with Mrs. Rawlings' Oklawaha and St. Johns.

Bigelow, in his study of Mrs. Rawlings' literary career, *Frontier Eden*, draws an extended comparison between *Cross Creek* and *Walden* as he discusses the composition of the former. "She had the same sensitivity as Thoreau to the flow of the seasons and, as he had done in *Walden*, used a cycle of the seasons as one of the main organizing devices of her" book.[2] She "meant the grove to be her Walden Pond, where like Thoreau she could front the essential facts of life, or perhaps more ac- curately, her Brook Farm, the place where she would achieve that holy harmony of mind and muscle which would produce the highest kind of human happiness. She soon discovered, as Haw- thorne did at Brook Farm, that the writing demanded precedence, and as soon as she was able to hire others, her own labors at the grove became either supervising or puttering, while she submitted more and more to the anguish of the typewriter." [3] And the reader "has the sense that she has put herself on record in this book much as Whitman or Thoreau had done in their books a hundred years earlier, believing as they did that the best approach to the universal is through the particular and personal." [4]

Bigelow's last reference seems to take into account an im- portant observation Mrs. Rawlings makes in regard to Thoreau, in her concluding chapter, "Who owns Cross Creek?" She reminds us that "Thoreau went off to live in the woods alone, to find out what the world was like." She concludes from this that "a man may learn a deal of the general from studying the specific, whereas it is impossible to know the specific by studying the general. For that reason, our philosophers are usually the most unpractical of men, while very simple folk may have a great deal of wisdom. . . . We at the Creek draw our conclusions about the world from our intimate knowledge of one small portion of it" (359–60).

And there is also the matter of authorial point of view to con- sider. In *Walden* Thoreau takes the "I" approach: "I should not talk so much about myself if there were any body else whom I knew as well" (*Walden*, "Economy"). In *Cross Creek* the "I"

approach gives way now and then to the "we" approach: "We
at the Creek draw our conclusions about the world . . ."; "We
at the Creek need and have found only very simple things" (3).

There is, finally, one additional matter. *Cross Creek*, like its
predecessor *Walden*, may be taken as a pastoral autobiography
that harks back in certain ways to the ancient Theocritan-Virgilian
tradition. A recent critical work on John Updike provides an
introduction to a consideration of *Cross Creek* as pastoral, although the latter work is not mentioned at all. Larry E. Taylor,
in *Pastoral and Anti-Pastoral Patterns in John Updike's Fiction*
(1971), reasons that "in the serious pastoral tradition, it is safe
to say that the subject is (1) people of low socio-economic
class, (2) living in simplicity and harmony, (3) against a background of rural nature." Taylor finds in this tradition "a conflict
between the sophisticated world the author (or character in
prose fiction) finds himself in, and the 'natural,' unsophisticated
world he longs for." This is "an essentially dramatic situation—
the kind of conflict necessary for such basic tensions as those
found in *Walden*, where Thoreau is pulled from the pencil factory
and literary salon to the banks of Walden" and where numerous
other authors and literary characters are also pulled back to
nature: Mark Twain, Huck Finn, Sinclair Lewis's Babbitt, Hemingway's Jake Barnes and Bill Gorton (in *The Sun Also Rises*),
Nathanael West's Miss Lonelyhearts, and Updike's Rabbit Ang-
strom. "Thus, alienation and loss of traditional beliefs and values
are stimuli for pastoral literature." [5]

The *ruri-urbi* dichotomy—is life better up at the villa or down
in the city?—can easily be overstated, as it is in Taylor's analysis.
And there is no need here to become embroiled in the issues of
geographical primitivism, the Noble Savage, and the teeter-totter
of pastoral and anti-pastoral elements in our literature. Still, *Cross
Creek* may be seen as a repudiation of one kind of sophistication
in favor of another kind of sophistication. "Having left cities
behind her," Mrs. Rawlings transferred her cultivated, reflective
sensibility to the North Florida woods where she could, for all
her occasional loneliness and frustration, make the best of two
worlds. Far above the other inhabitants of the Creek area in
education and refinement, she was a kind of reportorial visitor
from another planet. A great deal of the time, she wrote or
attempted to write, enjoying the status of one of Scribner's im-

portant authors. Celebrities visited her at the Creek and enjoyed her gourmet meals. On occasion she traveled to New York for an editorial conference or left the Creek far behind to get a change of scenery. For all its pastoral quality, *Cross Creek* reflects a wider range of experience than the bucolic or even the bucolic seen through urban eyes; there is the dimension of privilege that gives the book its particular character.

But the pastoral quality of *Cross Creek* (and *Walden*) calls up a related matter, the agrarian mythos, the mystique of the "field," the virtue of self-reliant cultivation of the land. "Insofar," Taylor points out, "as elements of the pastoral and anti-pastoral traditions exist in twentieth-century American fiction, they exist in some relation to a 'return to nature' motif, or a 'nature myth,' or an 'agrarian mystique.'" [6] And, when he uses the last term, Taylor means "a generalized American attitude toward nature, the land, and rural life—an attitude historically traceable and still current in large segments of American culture." [7]

Bigelow in *Frontier Eden* relates both the pastoral and the agrarian traditions to the backwoods way of life Mrs. Rawlings made famous. Penny Baxter (Jody's father in *The Yearling*), according to Bigelow, "falls squarely into the image of the idealized agrarian freeholder, which has been pervasive in American culture since the eighteenth century." Penny, "an independent, self-reliant yeoman farmer living in a great forest," represents "a frontier condition midway between the savagery of the mountain men and the corruptions of sophisticated society, that agrarian middle ground esteemed by Crèvecoeur and Jefferson as the ideal condition for human happiness."

Mrs. Rawlings' "use of this middle ground in her stories" leads Bigelow to identify "her with an important American pastoral tradition which has begun to be explored by scholars only in recent years"; by Henry Nash Smith in *Virgin Land* (1950), for example, and by Leo Marx in *The Machine in the Garden* (1964). Marx, extending Smith's earlier formulations, has demonstrated "the presence in American culture of a pastoral tradition deriving ultimately from Virgil." In *The Machine in the Garden*, Marx makes it clear that numerous writers in this country have made use of " 'the syntax of the middle landscape'—a symbolic setting or background for their stories which they locate somewhere between the corruption of effete civilization and the barbarism of the howling wilderness. . . . Among the major authors who have written American versions of the pastoral, utilizing this symbolic middle landscape, Marx discusses Jefferson, Thoreau, Twain, Hemingway, Frost, and Fitzgerald." Mrs. Rawlings "clearly belongs to this company." [8]

There can no longer be any doubt that it is high time for Mrs. Rawlings to be carefully reconsidered by American literary historians, most of whom have been almost entirely unaware of her contributions to our cultural heritage and her affinity with our more important homegrown naturalists of fact and fancy.

III   *Cooking/ Sharing/ Caring*

In the chapter "Visitors," Thoreau remarks, "You need not rest your reputation on the dinners you give. For my own part, I was never so effectually deterred from frequenting a man's house, by any kind of Cerberus whatever, as by the parade one made about dining me, which I took to be a very polite and roundabout hint never to trouble him so again. I think I shall never revisit those scenes." But, as for Mrs. Rawlings, it may be said that her cooking graced her life. Her newspaper poems—in the mid-1920s—about the "romance in pots and pans" have already been mentioned. In a culinary note published in 1939 she exulted, "I write as an introvert, attempting to turn an intangible loveliness into a tangible conception. But I cook as an extrovert singing at the top of my lungs, in ecstasy and the certainty of fulfillment." [9] Again and again in her fictions she describes a woman, usually on a farm, who loves to cook and whose culinary achievements have to be detailed for the reader.

Chapter 17 of *Cross Creek*, "Our daily bread," a précis of her life as an open cookbook, gives us some idea of her socio-esthetic-gastronomic creed. "I hold the theory that the serving of good food is the one certain way of pleasing everybody. . . . Cooking is my one vanity and I am a slave to any guest who praises my culinary art." As for how she came to be so intensely interested in fine cooking, her "recognition of cookery as one of the great arts was not an original discovery, but it is as important a one for the individual woman as the discovery of love." Both her mother and her maternal grandmother [10] happened to have been outstanding cooks. "But there was a taint on [her mother's] art, for she did not consider it a notable accomplishment and she refused to teach me. Also, she worked so hard at it, with so little joy, no matter how capable a maid stood at her side, that she was exhausted, with a migraine headache, when a special feast was ready, and could not touch any of the magnificent dishes" (206).

Young Marjorie Kinnan, watching her mother's cooking feats, assumed that they were due to instinct and that she herself had also inherited the ability. But she found out otherwise. After her marriage, it was harshly brought home to her that she did not have the gift. One day her mother-in-law sent her the *Boston Cook Book*. Studying it, she now found herself able to reproduce her mother's unwritten recipes. And over the years she often felt that, if she were penniless but adequately healthy, she would enjoy supporting herself by being a cook. As for the new land she came to call her home, "the new foods that I found in Florida were a challenge and I have learned more about cookery in my years at the Creek than in those that preceded them" (207).

It was natural, therefore, that she would eventually collect all of her recipes in a book that would be laced together with "Cross Creek Menus" and homey conversation about the joys of cooking. The work was published in 1942 under the title *Cross Creek Cookery*, and was embellished with illustrations and a number of recipes for out-of-state dishes. Despite its short length, the book was enormously successful. The brief concluding section, " 'Better a Dinner of Herbs,' " is unforgettable.

Taking her text from Proverbs 15:17, "Better is a dinner of herbs where love is, than a stalled ox and hatred therewith," she explained clearly just what her culinary creed was. If she ate alone, leftovers or make-do food would be her dish. "It never occurs to me to turn out an elaborate meal without company to partake." There are two prerequisites for felicitous table gatherings: (1) the food, whatever its nature, must be prepared with care, willingness, and imagination; (2) the guests, whoever they are, "must be conscious of their welcome. Formal dinners of ill-assorted folk invited for the sole purpose of repaying social obligations, are an abomination."

Mrs. Rawlings felt that "the breaking together of bread, the sharing of salt, is too ancient a symbol of friendliness to be profaned." While they dine, "the assembled group stands for a little while as a safe unit, under a safe roof, against the perils and enmities of the world." Since this group will separate and be scattered, "for this short time, let them eat, drink and be merry." Not only are guests "acutely conscious of the spirit in which they have been invited," but even the immediate family feels the mood of the kitchen, so to speak. "The mother or wife who grumbles over the planning and cooking of meals, taints the very vitamins." What matters, in essence, is "the delight of friends and family in being together" (217–18).

One pictures a dinner party for two, both of them proud, touchy, introverted, and solitary intellectuals who prefer simple, rural surroundings to noisy, urban ones. Each is a writer, and each is familiar with the other's work. The hostess speaks: "I believe you wrote, Sir, that if you dined out occasionally as you always have done and doubtless shall have opportunities to do again, it was frequently to the detriment of your domestic arrangements? Surely, Sir, that does not seem very encouraging to a host." Her guest replies: "I did say that, Ma'am, but I believe in observing *some* of the customs of the country. As you said yourself, there's no greater offense in the rural South than refusing a meal. And . . ." (here a sudden glint of shrewd practicality comes into his eyes) ". . . if they don't get dyspepsia or stomach ulcers, anybody'd be pleased with dishes that are well-cooked and imaginative."

CHAPTER 7

An Alien's Progress, Ad Astra Per Aspera:

The Sojourner

I *An Alien Re-alienated*

MRS. RAWLINGS' last novel, *The Sojourner*, is markedly different from her other novels in that it does not concern the harsh, earthy existence of the Florida Crackers. The locale is upstate New York, where she was living—intermittently—during much of the composition of the book. Although *The Sojourner* is about people whose lives are dedicated to living on the soil and wresting a living from it, Mrs. Rawlings clearly was no longer in her element when she depicted their lives.[1] Her message comes through somehow, but the story is weak in many places, and the characterization is often flat—in fact, painfully unimaginative. Yet the reader finds himself, after finishing the book, coming back again and again to the message; for it touches the very basis of human existence.

On publication, *The Sojourner* had the recommendation to the reading public of having been chosen a Literary Guild selection. But somehow the novel seems not to have been very successful with a general audience or with the literary critics, particularly in the light of such earlier successes as *The Yearling* and *Cross Creek*. While Louis Bromfield stated that it was "a good novel" and "a solid novel," and that on occasion it contains "passages of inspired writing," [2] not many shared his opinion. Edward Weeks could not believe in the basic motivations of the major characters,[3] and Riley Hughes called the book "an astonishingly inept and wooden parable of the life of man, lacking in drama and confusing self-righteousness with goodness." [4] Julia Scribner Bigham, in her *Marjorie Rawlings Reader*, makes no mention of the novel whatever. And Bigelow's *Frontier Eden* disparages

The Sojourner: as "a noble attempt [on the author's part] to write the great American novel" it fails more than it succeeds, even when not read as realistic fiction but as allegory; it suffers from a forced plot, wooden characters, frequently sententious and turgid prose—the author's ambition was too large and the mode was alien to her.[5]

There is more than a little irony in this reference to an alien mode. Twice estranged from her native habitat, Mrs. Rawlings now produced a novel that dealt with a man who devoted all of a long life to his farm and his family, only to find himself at the end a part of neither one, alienated somehow from all he was in closest touch with, and forced to realize one of the bitterest truths of human experience: man's true roots are not in this earth.

II   *An Existentialist Novel Like* The Stranger?

A contemporary note is struck midway in *The Sojourner* with a reference to the desirability of one's being able to "do his thing." Tim McCarthy, a down-at-heels farmhand whose brother is an itinerant apple-tree seller, is comparing him with Asahel Linden's brother Benjamin, who had left the family farm many years before to seek his fortune in the Far West. They are, McCarthy says, "'good lads, both of them, good lads. A-doing of the thing they want to do, and that's important for a man, is it not? And I've not done it'" (161). It was characteristic of Mrs. Rawlings' own life-course that she generally managed to "do her thing" despite obstacles and frustrations, and also despite the fact that she was a female living a much more rugged life than most women of her background would ever wish to do.

After *Cross Creek* and *Cross Creek Cookery* were published in 1942, she developed the idea for a novel based to an extent on the life of her maternal grandfather Traphagen. During the latter part of the nineteenth century this man had farmed in southern Michigan. On a visit to an aunt in Michigan in August, 1943, Mrs. Rawlings was able to go through a vast amount of her grandfather's personal papers. These had the odd effect of simultaneously advancing her project through a plenitude of information and retarding her writing efforts through a glut of data.[6] Despite any number of personal hardships and writing blocks, she persisted in working on the book for something like a decade. Here, as in so many of her other writings, she was very personally involved in her material. In its own way *The Sojourner* represented to her a "land of heart's desire" just as strongly as did *The Yearling* or *Cross Creek.*

The Sojourner is a family-chronicle novel dealing with the Linden family, which operates a large farm in upstate New York [7] during the period from about the end of the Civil War to the late 1930s. On the death of Hiram Linden, the head of the family,[8] his widow Amelia is left to run the farm with only the help of her two sons: Benjamin, twenty-three; Asahel, twenty. She had long ago completely rejected her husband on the grounds that he was too cowardly to stand up to his own father and brother when they had betrayed him in a family agreement involving their farmland. Just as she has always loved Benjamin, whom she calls her "only true begotten son . . . conceived in love" (15), she has always hated Asahel, the biological result of an angry sexual attack on her by the infuriated Hiram.

After his father's funeral, Benjamin leaves the farm to seek his fortune in the West, and Amelia and Asahel are left desolate. Their hearts cry, " 'Son and brother, we cannot face life without you, because of love, never because of a living!' " (5). Asahel marries Nellie Wilson, the girl Benjamin has indifferently left behind, and settles down to running the farm and raising a family. Through the years the bereft Amelia grows more and more hard-bitten, solitary, and peculiar. And it becomes increasingly clear that Benjamin is never coming back and will continue to remain generally inaccessible, even by mail. Only on the rarest occasions does the family receive even the vaguest word of Benjamin's far wanderings and questionable activities.

Nellie, a sprightly and resourceful woman who is given on occasion to playing practical jokes (as was Mrs. Rawlings), loves cooking and caring for her family. She and Asahel rear a brood of five children, while Amelia remains grumpily indifferent or openly hostile. With the exception of the youngest, Doll, who is deeply attached to her father, their offspring are a sorry lot: materialistic, colorless, unintelligent. When Doll is about six, Amelia, who has harbored a paranoid jealousy toward the child since she was born, deliberately loses her in a blizzard, and the child perishes. Much as Asahel grieves, his sense of loss at

Benjamin's irremediable absence remains unaffected. Outside of Nellie, the only people who are not strangers to him are Tim McCarthy; an old Fisher Indian named Mink who is, significantly, the last of his tribe; and a band of gypsies who camp near the farm every year or so. Tim and Mink are like substitute fathers to Asahel, and the gypsies have practically made him one of their own.

The oldest Linden child, Nat, has been a money-worshipper almost since he was a toddler. When he attains young manhood, he becomes concerned that Asahel has never obtained title to the farm from the long-absent Benjamin, who is still technically the owner. He is disgusted with his father's simple trust that the farm is virtually his, despite the fact that Amelia could not convey the farm to him even if she wanted to, which she assuredly does not.

As the years pass, Asahel, who by and large continues to do well on the farm, experiences more losses: the deaths of his mother, his friends Tim and Mink, and his youngest son, Willis, a casualty of World War I. There are other heartbreaks too. Nat, who has become a vulgar, money-crazy tycoon in the Far West, brags to Asahel whenever he returns home for a visit about his ability to buy legislators and increase his money power. The next son, Arent, a spineless nonentity, has turned into Nat's unquestioning lackey. 'Melie, the daughter, enters into a marriage of convenience with a crude money-grubber who is even more unsavory than Nat. At last Nellie, who has been married to Asahel for more than sixty years, dies. Now Nat attempts, amiably but insistently, to gain control of the family estate so that he can parlay it into a fast and easy fortune. One day Asahel receives a letter from a woman in a San Francisco lodging house, telling him that his brother Benjamin is very ill and is asking for him. And so Asahel takes a train for the West Coast to have the reunion with Ben that he has been yearning for ever since Ben had left home well over half a century before.

Asahel arrives in San Francisco and finds Ben, who is dying. In the short time available to them, they cover the sixty-odd years of separation. Ben gives his brother a deed to the family farm; he had been keeping the document all these years because he had wanted to show that he was a man of property. After asking Asahel to take him along when he returns to the New York farm, Ben has a sudden heart attack and dies.

To his sad brother now, "Nothing was different, [Ben] was no more lost to him than he had ever been. It came to him with a sharp knowledge that in his loneliness he was not alone. He thought, 'Every man has lost his brother'" (310). Asahel makes preparations to convey the farm not to his unworthy son Nat but to a Polish-Scandinavian family, the Rabaskis, whom he has settled on the land. There is a feeling of kinship between the Rabaskis and Asahel; young Jan Rabaski, in particular, regards him as a father-figure. Before going to San Francisco, in fact, Asahel had legally devised to the Rabaskis all the livestock and farm machinery and equipment to which he could validly claim title; and to Jan, "his only true though unbegotten son" (294), he had made over all of his cash holdings in the form of a trust fund. At that time he had bequeathed to Nat, whom he did not consider his son any more, the sum of five thousand dollars—the amount of the war insurance policy left by Willis. The other two Linden children were left nothing.

Flying back East alone, Asahel thinks of what has happened and about what it all might signify. Like Benjamin, "he, too, he recognized, had sought to find the unfindable. He had lost and sought a brother, and it was in the faces of all men he should have peered" (311). Then Asahel himself has a heart attack and is one with the stars.

There is a haunting loneliness throughout the novel: in its title, biblical epigraph (I Chronicles 29:15), the entire story line, and the very memorable concluding paragraph. The mood of the book suggests, in fact, not only loneliness but also the sadness resulting from both an unappeased hunger and a bereavement whose wounds refuse to heal. We might even say that the book is pervaded by an existentialist feeling.

The existential philosophy, in the words of the British writer Anthony Burgess, involves "the notion that man is only defined by perpetual emergence, becoming something else, fighting, presenting his thesis to some antithesis, perpetually in conflict, defining himself in fact as an emergent being." [9] Stated more familiarly, *existence is prior to essence*. All of which, if applied here, suggests that the protagonist of the story was definitely his own man and not an acted-upon individual passively allowing his predetermined design to actualize itself. Yet Asahel is the very embodiment of the plodding, self-contained man of the soil working his land throughout most of his waking hours for the length of his days. There is little romance and not very much in the way of existentialist crisis in his quiet life, even when he loses his loved ones over the years. He is clearly another example of one of Mrs. Rawlings' important character types: the heroic husbandman. What then is existential about Asahel?

William Barrett, in his well-known work on existentialism, *Irrational Man*, enumerates the themes which in his opinion "obsess both modern art and existential philosophy." These are: "the alienation and strangeness of man in his world; the contradictoriness, feebleness, and contingency of human existence; the central and overwhelming reality of time for man who has lost his anchorage in the eternal." [10] In calling attention to Barrett's important summary, the authors of the handbook *Backgrounds of American Literary Thought* extend the formulation as follows: "If we add to such themes the concept of a protagonist who must freely choose, in loneliness and anguish, that course of action which is for him the authentic life—and bear the full responsibility of his choice—we shall have formulated the general characteristics of a literature existentialist in spirit if not so by technical definition." [11]

From this standpoint, then, Asahel may be seen as something of an existential figure; and *The Sojourner* may be compared after a fashion with more easily recognizable existentialist novels. Barrett's first point is of special importance: "the alienation and strangeness of man in his world." For all its old-fashioned, family-chronicle plot, for all its stilted and spiritless dialogue, *The Sojourner* has the ingredients for an existentialist story; and its hero—with his loneliness and sense of alienation—*seems* to step out of the pages of Dostoevsky or Camus. But there is a special irony, involving a paradox of definition.

Despite surface similarities, what really sets *The Sojourner* apart from such well-known existentialist works as Camus's *The Stranger* has already been hinted at. Asahel's essential alienation and rootlessness are closely related to his deep-rootedness to a particular location and to a particular social group. Asahel does not—until the very end of his life—have a valid claim to the farm, and thus he is in a painfully ambiguous position in regard to it. And he is a kind of outsider in his own family, to which he has also devoted a lifetime of service. His beloved brother leaves home early, never to return. His mother has always hated him and causes the death of his dearest child. His other children merely tolerate him, at best. As for his wife Nellie, she had never really loved him. " 'She never got over loving you, Ben,' " he tells his dying brother, and Ben replies, " 'Nellie didn't love anybody, Ase' " (307).

Measure a man by his sense of loss, one thinks, in reading the story of this man's life. Asahel's predicament—which can never be resolved while he lives—is that something like a deep feeling of personal loss, perhaps a painful lack of affection from his closest kin (he repulses at least two of them—his mother and his son Nat—by his homeliness) impoverishes his life. Nothing seems to belong to him—neither wife, children, land, nor house: "He was a stranger."

But this feeling makes him ashamed of himself: "He had every-thing a man could ask for. He wondered in horror if his adora-tion of Nellie was not love at all, but only the panic of a drowning man clinging to his rescuer. For she was rescue, truly. She was the bridge between his isolation and the warmth and safety of life itself." Perhaps the one loss that counted was that of his brother Benjamin. "Or was it his destiny to be always unfilled and lonely? He felt himself coming closer to a truth, and as his heart beat faster, the truth evaded him." Asahel yearns to draw his small son "Nat close against him, to say, 'We have both arrived strangely on earth and shall depart strangely, and we are related for the moment, so let us try to speak together, alien as we may appear one to the other' " (166–67). This is the heart of Asahel's (existentialist) difficulty throughout the story. He can never get close enough to anyone (except Doll, who dies a very early death) to connect—to develop the feeling that he is really a part of things—to get rid of "his loneliness in the midst of love and plenty" (158).

Barrett's first point, about "the alienation and strangeness of man in his world," is followed by a reference to "the contra-dictoriness, feebleness, and contingency of human existence." Until Asahel attains old age, he remains firm in his decision to spend his life on the farm—in fact, to go no farther away than a nearby town—despite all: the remonstrances of his family, the chance that travel might lead him to Benjamin, and the fact that "his feet had itched all his life to walk on stranger roads" (253). His choice of what was for him the *authentic life* yielded far less in the way of satisfaction than of loneliness and anguish, but he never has any serious thought of selecting some other course of action. Once, briefly, sometime before Nellie's death, he expresses a willingness to move to one of the nearby towns on her account, but nothing comes of this.

They were only *dreams*, his notions about peering into foreign lands all over the globe, and the highest mountain ranges, "and high above these, up into interstellar spaces, so dazzling that he might be unable to face it if he found it, the home he yearned for, the true and final home that was not and never had been nor could be, the old Linden farm near Peytonville" (253–54). This description is a foreshadowing of the memorable last paragraph in the book, describing Asahel's feelings as he succumbs to a heart attack: "It had been so brief a sojourn, not even a full century. He had been a guest in a mansion and he was not ungrateful. He was at once exhausted and refreshed. His stay was ended. Now he must gather up the shabby impedimenta of his mind and body and be on his way again" (313). This passage is a final underscoring of the frailty, uncertainty, and essential dependence of Asahel's life on earth.

Mrs. Rawlings selected as the epigraph of her novel a verse from I Chronicles, 29:15. "For we are strangers before thee, and sojourners, as were all our fathers: our days on the earth are as a shadow, and there is none abiding." The entire story is expressive of the Old Testament theme of the precariousness of being on foreign soil, "an alien in a strange land" (Exodus 18:3). But the specific existentialist content of *The Sojourner* becomes more apparent when the novel is compared with another American novel that appeared ten years later—Kurt Vonnegut, Jr.'s *Cat's Cradle*, an attack on the use of the atom bomb in World War II.

The key concept of *Cat's Cradle* is of the greatest importance in an understanding of *The Sojourner*. Humanity, Vonnegut declares, is organized into special groups for a special purpose. Each of these groups or teams—Vonnegut uses the term *karass*—is intended to accomplish God's will, "without the members ever discovering what they are doing." And the *karass* is not concerned with conventional groupings: national, familial, organizational, etc. The corollary of the *karass* is the *granfalloon*, a false team held together by a meaningless label, that is definitely not instrumental in actualizing God's will. The members of a *granfalloon* are thrown together by accidental circumstances; but, despite superficial elements held in common, they do not belong together. The members of a *karass* are thrown together "for no very logical reasons," but they do belong together. Clearly, as Vonnegut blends theodicy with espionage lore (secret agents, teamwork through the "broken pieces of a puzzle," etc.), he is showing us how limited and even undesirable the whole *team* notion may be under certain conditions.

In *The Sojourner*, Asahel's entire life may be seen as a constant groping for the other members of his supposed *karass* and as a protracted and self-defeating entanglement with his associates in a *granfalloon*. Insofar as there is any hint of social purpose in Mrs. Rawlings' novel, it appears that property rights and family ties keep individuals working closely together in teams. But the entire notion of property, whether real or personal property, turns out to be a chimera and a stumbling block to the spirit. And family ties are revealed as pernicious fetters which man continues to wear at his peril—that is, bloodline family ties. Asahel really seems to be in tune with the cosmos only when he is with his adoptive kin: Tim McCarthy, Mink the Fisher Indian, the gypsies, and, most significantly, his tenants the Rabaskis. (There is nothing, Vonnegut points out, against our attempting to find out the limits of our *karass* and what kind of work God wants us to do; but, he adds, such searches cannot help but be incomplete.)

Asahel, then, is an existentialist hero who spends his life struggling to realize himself in his work and (sometimes ignoring logic and the demands of family) to establish a meaningful social relation. His efforts are often hampered and they may sometimes be tentative and uncertain; frustration is his frequent reward. But, far from being a total failure, Asahel's life has a certain grandeur, an imposing agrarian stature. In the very fact that his reach for spiritual fulfillment exceeded his grasp, he vindicates himself as a man.

III   *"A religious feeling that will probably be missed"*

One of the most significant features of *The Sojourner* was commented on by Mrs. Rawlings in a letter to the Reverend Arthur MacGillivray, S.J., written on September 20, 1952, not long before *The Sojourner* was published. The book, she said, has "a religious feeling that will probably be missed entirely by the average reader." [12] Since the novel is so concerned with land-*holding* (as opposed to land ownership), the transitoriness of man's stay on earth, and his relationship with some unfathomable divine plan—which is veiled from him while he lives on earth—the reader might imagine that Mrs. Rawlings had in mind something like what George Meredith intended when he wrote: "Our life is but a little holding, lent/ To do a mighty labour. We are one/ With heaven and the stars when it is spent/ To serve God's aim. Else die we with the Sun." A much more likely source of the novel's "religious feeling" is the all-pervasive brotherly attachment of Asahel to the absent Benjamin.

Another source is the concept of time and Asahel's attitude toward time. Mrs. Rawlings handles this complicated and sophisticated matter of time-awareness in such a way as to make it one of the significant features of the story. We must recall here William Barrett's third point of comparison between modern art and existential philosophy: "the central and overwhelming reality of time for man who has lost his anchorage in the eternal." Throughout much of *The Sojourner*, Asahel clearly senses this reality. By itself, of course, this time-awareness does not signify his having lost his grasp of the eternal. Up to a certain point in his life, time is felt to be a kind of ineffable unity which in effect mirrors the eternal.

When Asahel is still a fairly young man, he and his wife Nellie discuss their youngest child, Doll. Nellie comments about how strange it is that things change the way they do over the years: " 'The time jumps like a rabbit. Thinking we'd lose Doll, and now she's a big girl. You worrying about me, and Willis making no trouble at all. All of it in jumps.' " Someday, she supposes, having grown children will seem as queer as having new children. Then a remarkable passage follows about Asahel's quite opposite view, which may remind some readers of Thomas Wolfe's time-river image:

He was troubled by his feeling about time. It seemed to him that he had always known that he and Nellie would have children from their love. He had seen them from babyhood to manhood and womanhood as a consecutive flow, like the stream that ran from Pip Lake, under the willow trees and the wooden bridge, to join Long Lake, to flow in turn to the Meshawk River, which, he knew, joined other rivers and ran at last to the sea. He stood off at a distance and saw his remotest ancestors side by side with his farthest descendants.

He wondered if he had an unnatural point of view. Time for him was not marked off in jumps, as Nellie expressed it. It was not clearly marked and definite, it was all one, sometimes relative but forever whole. All life seemed to him contained in the beginning and the end, if there had ever been a beginning and if there would ever be an end. Time was, must be, timeless. As from a great enough height a land-scape would show no detail, so from a far enough distance all time would be seen to exist simultaneously. He felt this in his inner mind and spirit. (152–53)

Bigelow's comments throw additional light on this view of Asahel's when the critic speaks of Mrs. Rawlings' quasi-religious "cosmic consciousness" and likens it to the pantheism of Whitman or to the oversoul of the Transcendentalists. Bigelow refers to her "awareness that birth, growth, and death are one and good, and that the life which moved the stars was the same life which breathed through the forest and beat in her own heart."[13] She conceived of God, Bigelow points out, "as a great Life running through all things which was made up of individual lives as the ocean is made up of individual drops of water. In *The Sojourner* her representative man, Ase Linden, actually uses this Emersonian metaphor as he speculates about the nature of God. Her own contemplation of God always started with the natural world around her, then like Ase Linden she almost always raised her eyes to the heavens and let her mind range through space to that other dimension of her pantheism which she called 'cosmic consciousness.' "[14]

It is only natural that Asahel's particular philosophy of time —which has been given expression in Western thought for at least two centuries—would be affected by personal vicissitudes and would give way at least temporarily to a more conventional outlook. This happens to Asahel in middle age after Doll has died and after he comes to learn about the ravages of the passing years. His gypsy friends return for a brief stay, and Asahel renews his friendship (and kinship) with them. He discovers that the old queen is dying, and he recalls his long-ago romance with her daughter, who is herself well along in years. "For himself, he felt old for the first time in his life. Too much had happened in too short a while. For once, he lost his sense of the all-embracing unity of time and recognized a milestone in his life" (228).

Another description of his normative time-sense is given near the end of the novel in the passage referred to by Bigelow dealing with the "drops of water" and with God as all-pervasive Life. Asahel is seventy-one, and he and Nellie are discussing retirement. Struck by his projections for the future, Nellie asks him how long he expects to live. Asahel admits that he hasn't given it much thought, but he imagines that he'll live forever. In that case, she replies, he'll have to do it alone; her one life has almost been the death of her. "He wondered if he could explain his sense of timelessness. He did not think of it as another life, nor yet quite an immortality of the same one" (271).

Asahel's belief is given its ultimate jolt when he is eighty, and his wife dies. Although he has been faced with bereavement too many times already to be confounded by it now, his tightly held world-view weakens. What had become of his little wife? Asahel's "sense of the oneness, the timelessness, of God, of Man, of Life, had failed him." With her roguish vigor, she seemed not to fit into the overall plan or into his philosophical theories. "She would reject the outer cosmic spaces, as she had rejected all thought of immortality of body or of spirit . . ." Then a restorative feeling comes to Asahel and supports him—the reflowing of nature's force after its ebbing. "Yet surely she was not lost entirely. Something of her would forever breathe with the lilacs, would give delight to other lovers on other windy springtime hills" [15] (284).

The conflicts Asahel undergoes in regard to his time-sense are resolved, after a fashion, at the very end of the story, when Mrs. Rawlings fantasizes a physical and psychological basis for harmonizing linear time with unitary time (or the condition of timelessness). Just before his heart attack, Asahel hears the airline stewardess say that the plane will continue to climb for half an hour and then level off. Asahel has been in a state of exhilaration, remembering his boyhood conversations with Mink and his thoughts of "walking barefoot across the Milky Way." So affected is he now by the sensation of flying that he stretches his arms out "like an angel on the wing." Some deep hunger within him is being appeased. If only this half hour could be stretched into five hundred years, so that he could go "to the core of the cosmos." Asahel recalls "his years of watching after the bird migrations."

This reflection leads to one of Asahel's most significant thoughts about man's puny efforts on earth—and to one of Mrs. Rawlings' most moving expressions of religious belief, an optimistic creed couched in terms of far-reaching space and time. "The battered planet he had seen under him could not last forever. Something in man was surely eternal, if only his awareness of eternity. . . . Man might be migratory, too. In his blood and bones there might stir the same blind avian impulse toward unknown places. Since man could not soar alone, he had evolved these miraculous instruments of flight, making ready for an ultimate home, aeons and aeons hence." Then, dying, he feels the additional pain of leaving the earth. Perhaps the space-colonists of the future will share his tenant-yearning: " 'Dear earth, place once of my abiding' " (312–13).

What might Mrs. Rawlings have written if she had lived to see on television the first *moonwalk* in 1969?

The Sojourner is in many ways an unusually strong expression of Mrs. Rawlings' outer life-style as well as of her inner life. Certain areas of the novel remain inaccessible to conventional modes of literary analysis, but they yield interesting insights when subjected to "psychological" criticism, particularly Jungian analysis, with its concern with archetypes and the racial unconscious. The following remarks, for example, from a book on Jungian psychology applied to a literary work—John Bunyan's *The Pilgrim's Progress*—are suggestive enough for our purposes here to be included without additional comment:

In dreams and myths, as well as in parable and allegory, man's inner life and the process of his inner development is almost constantly represented as a journey, a progress from one stage to the next. . . . The persons encountered on the way will represent personifications of his own unconscious psychic components: the wild beasts are his own untamed instincts; the dangerous mountains and rivers and so forth are the threats to the life of his soul, the conflicts with which he is beset in his life; and the goal is the final solution of these conflicts and the resolution of the enigma of the human being. In the relevant literature, this goal is variously described. Sometimes it is portrayed as some material value; at others it is represented as the reunion with a lost brother, who is really a part of one's self; or as enlightenment, a realization that one's own little separate entity is but a part of a greater whole; or perhaps that oneself is in truth identical with that supreme value which is variously named Self, Atman, or God.[16]

CHAPTER *8*

A Seeming Conclusion

I "Her Legacies Were Rich But Somehow Often Sad"

THE most obvious thing that Mrs. Rawlings has left us is a series of striking scenes of Cracker life in the North Florida woods in "the old time, the old days." Her discovery of the starkly beautiful Cracker world, which in her fiction is seen from the latter half of the nineteenth century onward, represents a genuinely valuable contribution to our national literature. But her universalizing of the Cracker conflicts with nature and society gives her fiction a special poignancy.

However, we must consider the significance for Mrs. Rawlings herself of her recognition that this Cracker world could take her "back to the frontier childhood of the American people" and to its simplicity and self-reliance. For her, this realization was, in Bigelow's words, "a true epiphany, flooding her consciousness with sudden illumination and a sense of urgency and excitement..." [1] In short, it made a writer out of her.

We may overlook her occasional depressions, the disagreeable breakup with her friend Zelma Cason, and her curious retreat to upstate New York—and take into account only the broader pattern. Mrs. Rawlings' life and work at the Creek and its larger environs reflected a "rightness" that extends beyond the environmental harmony she described in her autobiography. The Cracker world, with its hardships and quiet heroism, its slow-time traditions and its isolation from the mainstream of American life, gave her own private world the meaning it had to have in order to sustain her spirit. " 'When I settled here,' " she wrote the editor of *Scribner's Magazine* around 1931 after her "Cracker Chidlings" had been accepted, " 'and the delights of this Cracker material fired me with enthusiasm—material vital past any straight fiction I could ever create—I made up my mind that if I could not interest one of the few topnotch magazines in it, I would deliberately put the torment of unaccepted writing out of my life.'" [2] Her literary success, beginning in February, 1931, when "Cracker Chidlings" was published, marked the psychological transformation that had taken place within her. She was now appeased, as she had apparently not been earlier in her life, since the death of her father in 1913.

But the painful truth is that she really was not appeased enough. If being introduced to the Cracker world made it possible for her to write publishable fiction and to become something of a literary celebrity—and if her non-Cracker stories were often very poor—why then wasn't more of her Cracker fiction of a really high quality? What went wrong when she was secure in her natural habitat, writing about the people she knew best and sympathized with the most? Bigelow, who speaks of her limited range, argues that she required "the specific stimulus of experience to spark her imagination, and not any personal experience would do. Only the Florida years seemed to be viable artistically." [3] He compares her unfavorably with writers having the greatest imaginative power, such as William Faulkner and Henry James, who could, in his opinion, be stimulated by an almost unlimited range of human experience.

This critical judgment—particularly in the case of Henry James, who knew nothing of the physical relations between men and women—is highly debatable. As for Faulkner, he was steeped in a plantation-aristocracy tradition going back a number of generations and had, moreover, spent years listening to "old-timers," black and white, who reminisced about their battles with life. Given his "high verbal" mentality, which also involved a remarkable sensitivity to language, and his overriding passion to produce fiction (once he realized he was not cut out to be a poet), he could be expected to succeed brilliantly where other well-endowed literary aspirants might fail.

Mrs. Rawlings, despite her insistent need to write, and a certain degree of verbal aptitude, lacked the genealogical milieu for a really significant body of fiction. Her family-farm tradition (through the Traphagens) was not nearly enough to offset this limitation. True, it helped her produce The Sojourner, but that novel, for all its strengths, is an abstraction of farm life conceived almost in Platonic terms that carries the reader from a simple, dedicated farmer's struggles with crops and family to the farmer's soul-flight toward the distant stars. And, the dialogue in the book is painfully flat, revealing the author's lack of understanding of people separated from her by a psychic distance. The Florida Crackers, despite all she was able to write about them, were part of her sense-world for too brief a time. Because her roots in their world were, finally, too new and fragile, they could not nourish her creative powers well enough or long enough for her to realize anything like the full potential of those roots.

A greater degree of verbal skill might have carried her much farther. We might consider in this regard not only William Faulkner but, more importantly, O. Henry, who could bring to life a number of different geographical regions as well as that of his native South and do so on the basis of fairly modest roots. O. Henry had, like Faulkner, "internalized" the old Southern tradition of spellbinding, classics-influenced rhetoric. Thus, it was natural for him to use high-sounding oratory composed of learned, newly coined, colloquial, formal, and technical terms blended together with a special incantatory force. Lacking this unusual kind of word-power, which is by no means limited to Southern writers, Mrs. Rawlings struggled long and hard for results that were frequently modest at best.

As far as artistic imagination and literary inventiveness, touched on suggestively by Bigelow, it is regrettably true that Mrs. Rawlings was also deficient in this area. She did not explore the lives of very many Crackers (or for that matter, non-Crackers), nor did she go into much detail in regard to their inner experiences. Hers was essentially a surface coverage, although *The Yearling* is something of an exception. A number of her Cracker stories (for instance, *South Moon Under* and "Jacob's Ladder") are annals of family housekeeping—births, marriages, deaths, getting a living, local customs, feuds, encounters with federal agents—against the background of the North Florida woods. The non-Cracker stories, with the exception of *The Sojourner*, are generally strenuous commercial efforts and accordingly are not indicative of her best creative powers.

Such critical comments are not intended to depreciate Mrs. Rawlings' literary accomplishments; the intent is to touch on the evidences of her not being appeased *enough* by her Florida homeland or by any other region she may have used as a locale for her fiction. Her difficulties with dialogue, particularly, are a clear indication of her failure to be reached and satisfied by the people (that is, by a significant number of them) she encountered in these locales. Hating large communities and preferring near solitude, she divorced herself from a vital artistic source and thus partially defeated her own purpose in writing. Her occasional sojourns with Cracker families, the numerous contacts with whites and blacks that are recorded in *Cross Creek*, do not controvert this basic tendency. Mrs. Rawlings' beautiful sonnet "Having Left Cities Behind Me" (1935) is at once a measure of the purity of her private vision, and a foreshadowing of its long-range crippling effect on her art:

> Now, having left cities behind me, turned
> Away forever from the strange, gregarious
> Huddling of men by stones, I find those various
> Great towns I knew fused into one, burned
> Together in the fire of my despising. . . .[4]

But we think of any number of poets and fiction writers who prospered, artistically, in deep seclusion—Emily Dickinson, Robinson Jeffers, J. D. Salinger, James Gould Cozzens, for example. Do not many great writers cut themselves off from society so that they can be free to entertain their artistic muse? Hawthorne (for all his talk of the Unpardonable Sin of Pride), Melville, Faulkner, and how many countless others made themselves into literary artists by their habit of self-cultivation, of solitary brooding—loafing and inviting contemplation. Not a few of these, however, nourished their imaginations on a rich store of intense personal experience which apparently had to be "recollected in tranquillity." Moreover, this private feeding on what has been laid aside for later use cannot (in most cases) continue indefinitely. Eventual artistic starvation seems to be practically inevitable, as was the case with Salinger and Cozzens.

All well and good for Emily Dickinson to write, honestly and accurately: "The Soul selects her own Society—/ Then—shuts the Door/ To her divine Majority—/ Present no more—" Up to a point this kind of selectivity served Mrs. Rawlings well, and there is no denying that without it she could not have come into her own as a skilled chronicler of the Florida Cracker world. Yet there was for her the inescapable problem of diminishing returns, of the very low marginal utility value of continued solitude. This was to plague her, whether she realized it or not, throughout much of her literary career. It was, in fact, to reduce drastically her chances of achieving artistic greatness —despite her "bringing off" a few very fine stories and a small number of good stories, as well as a beautifully wrought autobiography.

Thus, if we consider her Cracker fiction—and not her best, but the flawed though quite promising stories—we find hints of first-rate artistic expression, embedded in a matrix of raw, inchoate story materials. The gaunt, ill-used farm woman of "Gal Young Un" should have been brought to life instead of left as a symbol and a suggestion. The destitute Cracker couple in "Jacob's Ladder" should have been endowed with a much greater degree of vitality, particularly since the actual girl who was the prototype for Florry had made such a profound impression on Mrs. Rawlings. The same is true of another character based on this girl, Allie Brinley in *Golden Apples*. And, irony of ironies, Lant Jacklin in *South Moon Under*, one of the author's most important young boy idealizations, is largely a paper-doll figure. To judge from these and other works, it was extremely difficult for her to project her dramatis personae from the recesses of her mind onto the printed page so that they could enter the consciousness of her readers.

Mrs. Rawlings made very candid remarks about her tribulations as a writer and about the shortcomings of some of her literary efforts. Since she realized that her writing turned out unsatisfactorily now and again, it may well be that a feeling of artistic frustration, drawn out over the years, operated to affect her adversely, sapping her energies, her self-confidence, her social attitudes, and her resilience to life's stresses and strains. Was she, more than most other highly talented American writers of the 1930s and 1940s, caught up in an excruciating vicious circle from which she could never break free? Throughout her adult life, she seemed to be filled with a curious discontent and pent-up hostility; however, on infrequent occasions, she evinced happiness and even conviviality, but only for a relatively short interval. Her mood in many ways matched her literary creations,

and the pessimism or unrealistic optimism in them marked the
limits of her artistic, social, and also emotional resources. Yet,
she felt more deeply than most; and, when she was "working
well" (as Hemingway might have put it), this sensitivity showed
in her writing. It is a pity that she allowed numerous stories
resulting from her unhappy periods to be published.

II "No Tale Is Ever Told, No Portrait Ever Drawn"

There is no easy way to sum up Mrs. Rawlings' life and work
of the 1930s to the early 1950s. Unfair as it would be to average
the literary quality of her output, it would also be unfair to
draw hasty conclusions about her permanent contribution to
American literature. But the question arises, was she, at least,
an important minor Regionalist of the middle period of the twentieth century? Her own serious reservations about regional literature are recorded in a "position paper" of 1940, "Regional Literature of the South"; and academic commentary about her views
has been provided by Bigelow in *Frontier Eden* and also by me
in *Kansas Quarterly*,[5] a quite different approach to Mrs. Rawlings
being taken by each of us. What seems to be of greater significance than her so-called regionalism is her peculiar set of
sensitivities, her distinctiveness as a suffering (and sometimes
rejoicing) literary person who, in the final analysis, defies all
labels and attempts at evaluation.

Mrs. Rawlings responded to rhythms that most people are
unaware of or tend to misinterpret: the distant drum to whose
beat she moved was often beyond the range of common hearing.
Her soul selected its own society and the society of others with
rare discrimination. Indicative as Mrs. Rawlings' personal writings are, her other writings also reveal something of her strange
sensitivity, the distinctive cadence of "vibrations" that make her
worth studying. It is easy enough, but hardly worth the doing,
to give her credit for one Pulitzer Prize novel, a good autobiography, and a host of less significant works, mostly about the
Florida backwoods. What deserves closer attention is the "line"
that her fiction took.

If we look again at her four novels, and certain of her short
stories, we find that the human struggle, as she depicts it in her
fiction, has the effect of a spinal column in being a flexible

source of strength that is supportive of the solitary sojourner on earth. But sooner or later something goes wrong—an intervertebral cartilage becomes displaced, so to speak—and the crippling force resulting from this mischance is felt throughout the rest of the story. This "slipped disk" picture of things is entirely different from Thomas Hardy's tragic view of life, in which an *ironic* Fate constantly frustrates poor God-forgotten earthlings struggling vainly on a blighted star.

Hardy's characters and their author constantly complain about the injustices of life, the ironic miseries that make a wretched human existence so hard to endure, but Mrs. Rawlings' characters (and their author) incline more to a stoic acceptance. In the words of Penny Baxter, they " 'take it for their share and go on.' " A number of the important female characters, Ora Baxter and Amelia Linden, for example, react less maturely; they are frequently neurotic, fretful, and almost impossible for people to tolerate. But, even in such instances, we find no consistent philosophy (as we do in Hardy) of the hopelessness of the human condition.

What is this "slipped disk" effect? In *South Moon Under,* a sturdy patriarch named Lantry settles in the Big Scrub country, so that he can farm and raise his family in peace. But he had once killed a man, and he must now spend his life in comparative isolation from human society. At the end of the story, his grandson Lant kills his treacherous cousin Cleve and—because she actually gives herself to him—takes up with Cleve's widow, Kezzy. Brushing Lant's confession of murder aside, Kezzy indicates that it is no news to her: " 'I reckon you had it to do' " (132). As they start their new life together, with Kezzy's two children by Cleve, Lant thinks to himself (bringing the story full circle), " 'The law's like to come up with me yet' " (334). If this seems a strange, unnatural union and a weird conclusion to an unhappy domestic situation, we should consider "Gal Young Un." This tale deals with the rejected, aging wife of a young rakehell and the way in which she gets rid of her husband when he discards his latest "love," a scrawny little "gal" he brought home one day for his wife to take care of. After throwing him out, and his girl too, the wife relents and takes the "gal young un" back in, intending (we are led to assume) to act as a kind of stepmother to her. In Mrs. Rawlings' fiction, the "tie that binds" is a very special kind of bond; it has something of the quality of a blessing and of an anathema at the same time.

Golden Apples, to take another example, is about the deep emotional attachment of a brother and sister who are also isolated in the Florida woods. The sister is seduced by an exiled Englishman in whose house she and her brother are living as servants, and she later (after a forced wedding to the Englishman) dies in premature childbirth. Stricken, having lost the only woman he will ever love (as someone points out in the story), the brother lays instant claim to a dull-witted girl from a village some distance away, and then quickly marries her, in a scene reminiscent of the early "L'il Abner" comic strip. She begins to act like a dutiful, affectionate wife; but her new husband, who earlier had delivered a moving oration on proper and improper love between man and woman, only abuses her in a brutal but ludicrous manner. In "The Shell," a short story about a union between a normal and a dull-witted individual—during World War II—the husband is missing in action, and his mentally retarded wife, obeying his earlier injunction "to watch the sea, for he would be there," [6] goes looking for him where the cool waves are—and is soon swallowed up by them.

In *The Yearling,* we find a special instance of the calamitous tie that binds, the "slipped disk" of human experience. Here a lonely and solitary boy just entering upon his teen years lives in an almost inaccessible forest clearing with his stern and disagreeable mother and his soft-spoken, noble-souled father (to whom he is deeply attached). The boy is given a fawn for a pet, and this young deer becomes his alter ego—almost, literally, a part of him. But the fawn—grown now into a yearling—begins destroying the family's crops; and there is no foolproof way either to keep it penned up or to free it. So the boy's parents force him to kill his beloved deer. The novel ends by hinting at a most painful question: *what price survival* if man must destroy what seems like a vital part of himself, and if practically no other creature ever has to face this kind of test?

In Mrs. Rawlings' last novel, *The Sojourner,* we find a series of harsh, painful wrenchings resulting from the perversion of normal human affection. All through this story, the tie that binds also fastens upon its objects misery and sorrow. The book shows all too clearly that *natural* affiliation is not the only kind of affiliation that really matters, certainly not the best kind of "binding" available to sojourners on this earth. The son whom the mother loves leaves the family farm forever (although he retains the title to it). The other son, hated by the mother (because he had been begotten by her rejected husband), stays on the farm—mourning his lost brother as his mother mourns her lost son. He marries his brother's discarded sweetheart and has five children, only the youngest of whom has any deep feeling for him. This child dies in a snowstorm, as a result of his mother's psychotic hatred of him.

At the end of a long life, after he has "written off" his surviving children as worthless and has adopted (figuratively) one of the sons of the tenant on his farm, he is finally reunited with his brother. The latter, who is on his deathbed, gives him the title to the family farm. But he too is not far away from death; and now, ironically, he is made to realize that his wife, who had died somewhat earlier, had actually never loved him. In sum, his many decades of struggle to work the farm and to rear a large family have been more or less in vain. He has never had any *real* home or any certain knowledge or even any *real* family ties.

Another story ("Jessamine Springs," 1941), which is far more pointed in its theme than *The Sojourner*, also contains a protagonist who has difficulty establishing ties with others; in this case, no one wants him, and he is a kind of "Outcast of the Universe" (in Hawthorne's phrase). The man is the Reverend Thomas Pressiker—his tale is in the "ludicrous clergyman" tradition—and he is a tragicomic misfit lost between two worlds: the world of Christian belief and service, and the world of "regular fellers" who talk and act normally. Pressiker's ties to each of these worlds were never made fast, and so they are merely tenuous links which frustrate him and set all his efforts at naught.

What do Mrs. Rawlings' stories seem to be saying? Man, the frail, struggling sojourner on this inhospitable planet, will *not* realize his fondest hopes and wishes—he will get knocked down by life—as Penny Baxter puts it—yet will have no choice but to get up again and keep on going every time the blow falls. Like Penny, again, he will be hurt at least "once too often" by his fellow humans. In this elemental story pattern (seen very clearly in "Jacob's Ladder," for example), with its overtones of the great folktales, there appears to be a deeply personal feature that characterizes Mrs. Rawlings' own life: the failure of the romantic dream. Many well-known novels have been constructed around this theme: Cervantes' *Don Quixote*, Flaubert's *Madame Bovary*, Fitzgerald's *The Great Gatsby*. And countless writers, including George Meredith, Ernest Hemingway, and Sherwood Anderson, have developed numerous variations on this idea. Yet in Mrs. Rawlings' life and in her writings there is a special significance in the fact that things man has such high hopes for, that man invests so much emotional capital in, do *not* work out in the end.

If her problems and her particular "vibrations" must always remain somewhat obscure to us, the subject is at least worth mentioning briefly. Not only did they shape her literary productions and direct her career as a writer, but they continue to provide an important key to the way she interpreted the world to a vast number of readers who, like herself, are temporary sojourners on this disappointing planet.

But Mrs. Rawlings' melancholy, her tragic view of life, were not *merely* reflections of a solitary writer's dedication to her art. Nor were they *primarily* due to her disappointment because of her artistic failures. Bigelow, in attempting to explain her sadness, quotes a remark of hers about her being in a state of despair when she was not in contact with a cosmic current (of artistic inspiration). And he compares her with a number of other very well-known American writers with this kind of dark mood, who (just as she did) became addicted to alcohol in order that they might be able to bear the pain: Fitzgerald, Lardner, Hemingway, Faulkner; he might have added Sinclair Lewis as well. Then, considering Jung's theories about "the artist possessed by a *furor poeticus* so great it consumes the vessel which contains it," Bigelow admits that she was not a great enough genius for such artistic-psychological pain: "Hers was much more the pathos of the artist whose divine fire would not burn brightly enough." [7] Bigelow's view, in a nutshell, is that "this dark strand in her life was similar to what is now fashionably called existential despair and apparently had no specific content except that she suffered most from it when the writing was going badly." [8] We must disagree strongly, for to go along with this view would be to take Mrs. Rawlings' works at their face value and, by scanning, disregard them as the critics have done.

We must measure each man (writer) by his sense of loss. Let us ignore the truism that, if there had been no loss, there might not have been any writing. The loss may occur very early in life, but in any event if it is really *felt* as a loss it will work on the writer to make him feel insecure and perhaps inferior, at odds with his environment no matter how adjusted he appears. There was Sinclair Lewis, losing his mother at a very early age, having an unsightly facial appearance, and always being made to feel—by his older brother, a successful doctor— that he was not nearly as good as he should have been. There was Ernest Hemingway, a young scapegrace who would always feel that he was not up to par as a fighter and as a man—that is, as a writer—so that not even his great physical accomplishments and risks, and his global literary fame, would be enough to keep him from finally taking his own life. There were Thomas Wolfe and his absent father—Jack London and his unreachable, unknowable one. There was Scott Fitzgerald, mooning over the golden girl he could never really keep. Finally, Mrs. Rawlings, and the one link she might have had, but didn't, with the harsh huddling of men by stones and trees and rivers: a small boy who was and would forever remain her own. A small boy like her dead father or long-absent brother had once been, a small boy like Jody Baxter who would understand what it meant to take life's shattering blows and rise up again, who could in fact do that very thing *for her* as no one else could (and certainly not she herself), and thus show her the only real way to endure this earthly sojourn.

On the Difficulty of Reconstructing the Life of
Marjorie Kinnan Rawlings from Scattered Fragments
for a Biography

To outwit time and place,
To summon back a shape whose here and now
Erase this interval of slack:
A moment's miming for the gape and blink,
A hum of used-to-be . . .
The frailest counterfeit to track.

    To summon back the dream we should have kept,
    Or step aside for once,

Rejecting time's dread course . . .
Who so adept, to catch an interdicted gleam
By force, and ride
On wishes where no path is spread?
To bear awhile love's sharpest pain,
Love's most pervasive bliss,
Ignoring or at best enduring all
That runs amiss, and in that style
No fear of loss or hope of gain
Deters from the abyss.

No tale is ever told, no portrait ever drawn.
Some blurs of memory leavings hold our mind,
Then pale. And when they're gone, what then
Occurs? But nothing's really finished,
Come what may, and in
That better life around the bend, *no end*!
A man becomes a boy again, and wishes
Spring up clear, and
'Spite of nature's way—all rules now
Set at naught—
A fawn comes from a deer.

Notes and References

Chapter One

1. This poem, composed by me, appeared originally in *The American Poet* (Jan.–March, 1970), p. 33. Copyright 1970, W. S. Tremble. The poem was also anthologized in *The Golden Quill Anthology 1970* (Francestown, N.H., 1970), p. 21.

2. Thom Wilkerson, "Cross Creek Area Gets More Visitors," *Ocala* (Florida) *Star-Banner*, January 4, 1965, p. 12. I wish to thank Miss Lois Dickson of McIntosh, Florida, for sending me a copy of this paper.

3. Jane Quinn (feature story on Marjorie Kinnan Rawlings), *St. Augustine* (Florida) *Record*, March 15, 1942. Kinnan Family archives, Phoenix, Arizona.

4. Ernest L. Meyer (book review of *South Moon Under*), *Madison* (Wisconsin) *Capitol-Times*, March 2, 1933; quoted in Gordon E. Bigelow, *Frontier Eden: The Literary Career of Marjorie Kinnan Rawlings* (Gainesville, Fla., 1966), p. 9.

5. Letter to me from Mrs. Robert Wohlforth, Ridgefield, Connecticut, May 5, 1972.

6. Interview with Marjorie Kinnan Rawlings, *Rochester* (New York) *Times-Union*, June [n.d.], 1926. Kinnan Family archives, Phoenix, Arizona.

7. Kinnan Family archives, Phoenix, Arizona. See also Bigelow, *op. cit.*, p. 12.

8. Bigelow, *op. cit.*, p. 16.

9. *Ibid.*, pp. 25–26.

10. *Ibid.*, p. 31.

11. This statement is taken from a newspaper account of Mrs. Rawlings' address "Fact and Fiction," presented before the Kentuckiana Institute in Louisville on October 4, 1939. Written by Molly Clowes, the news story appeared in the *Louisville Courier-Journal*, October 5, 1939, p. 1.

12. Sarah Shields Pfeiffer, "Only One Road to Success—Says Mar-

jorie Kinnan Rawlings," *Christian Science Monitor*, September 4, 1940. Kinnan Family archives, Phoenix, Arizona.

13. Harry Evans, "Marjorie Kinnan Rawlings: Part Two," *The Family Circle*, May 14, 1943, p. 28.

14. Harry Evans, "Marjorie Kinnan Rawlings: Part One," *The Family Circle*, May 7, 1943, pp. 10–11.

15. Bigelow, *op. cit.*, pp. 40, 41, 42, 44.

16. Marjorie Kinnan Rawlings, letter to Misses Wilmer and Grace Kinnan, Cross Creek, Hawthorne, Florida, May 30, 1946. Kinnan Family archives, Phoenix, Arizona.

17. Bigelow, *op cit.*, pp. 44, 45, 46.

18. Letter to me from Mr. O. L. Van Horne, Cooperstown, New York, May 11, 1965.

19. *Utica* (New York) *Observer-Dispatch*, September 2, 1951, p. Bl.

20. Letter to Misses Grace and Wilmer Kinnan from Mrs. Lillian May, Jacksonville, Florida, January 7, 1954. Kinnan Family archives, Phoenix, Arizona.

21. Letter to Misses Grace and Wilmer Kinnan from Mr. Norton Baskin, December 23, 1953. Kinnan Family archives, Phoenix, Arizona.

22. Letter to Misses Grace and Wilmer Kinnan from Mr. Norton Baskin [n.d.]. Kinnan Family archives, Phoenix, Arizona.

Chapter Two

1. Paul Brooks, "Oklawaha: 'The Sweetest Water-Lane in the World,' " *Audubon*, LXXII (July, 1970), 36.

2. This discussion of the moon's effect on the sex of the birthling is to be found early in the second half of chapter 3 of "Book First: The Three Women" in Hardy's *Return of the Native*.

3. Close kinship between Lant Jacklin in *South Moon Under* and Jody Baxter in what was eventually to be *The Yearling* is foreshadowed in the letters (October 27, 1933, to November 15, 1933) of Mrs. Rawlings' editor (and mentor) at Scribner's, Maxwell E. Perkins. See *Editor to Author: The Letters of Maxwell E. Perkins*, edited by John Hall Wheelock (New York, 1950), pp. 83–86.

Chapter Three

1. Quoted in Bigelow, *Frontier Eden*, p. 135.

2. *The Nation*, CXLI (December 25, 1935), 750.

3. Eleanor Clark, *The New Republic*, LXXXV (December 4, 1935), 111.

4. Percy Hutchison, *The New York Times Book Review*, October 6, 1935, p. 3.

5. Julia Scribner Bigham, "Introduction," *The Marjorie Rawlings Reader* (New York, 1956), p. xvi.

6. Bigelow, *op. cit.*, pp. 17, 134.

7. *Ibid.*, p. 18.

8. But it is not possible to accept at face value Bigelow's entire statement (*Frontier Eden*, p. 2) that "since she was chiefly a plain-spoken writer, not a conscious symbolist except in her last novel, she has attracted little attention from critics interested in ironies, ambiguities, and symbol-chasing." Plain-spoken she may have been, but there is actually a great deal of irony and diversified symbolism in much of her fiction.

9. Purley represents the actual town of Island Grove, as Tordell's hammock land estate is drawn from Mrs. Rawlings' own citrus grove at Cross Creek. For a more extended geographical comparison, see Bigelow, *op. cit.*, p. 74. There are also useful maps in his book.

10. In the third section of his *Letters from an American Farmer* (1782), Hector St. John de Crèvecoeur, a French adventurer who had spent some years as a planter in New York, celebrated the American's newness in the following terms: "What, then, is the American, this new man? He is neither an European nor the descendant of an European; hence that strange mixture of blood, which you will find in no other country. . . . *He* is an American, who, leaving behind him all his ancient prejudices and manners, receives new ones from the new mode of life he has embraced, the new government he obeys, and the new rank he holds." Cf. Bigelow, *op. cit.*, pp. 120–22, on the American myth of the "garden" and the archetypal frontier farmer, as treated in Henry Nash Smith's *Virgin Land* and Leo Marx's *The Machine in the Garden*, and in American literature generally, particularly in Mrs. Rawlings' *Golden Apples* and *The Yearling*.

11. Yet, to complicate the "age" problem further, Tordell is occasionally described as being older than the Floridians he is brought in contact with, even, in fact, Doctor Albury.

12. Bruce Jay Friedman, "23 Pat O'Brien Movies," in his story collection *Far From the City of Class* (New York, 1963), p. 215.

Chapter Four

1. Jody Baxter may be categorized all too easily as a "Good Bad Boy" or a "Good Good Boy" by critics concerned only with superficial signs: rebellion against Mother and the world of women, nominal obedience to parents, lighting out for the Territory instead of staying home, etc. It is unfair to the author's intention or to Jody, who defies labeling, to simplify his role in the story.

2. Quoted in a letter to me from Mrs. R. P. Jameson, New York, New York, January 29, 1965.

3. Kinnan Family archives, Phoenix, Arizona.

4. Jane Quinn, *St. Augustine* (Florida) *Record,* March 15, 1942.

5. Harry Evans, "Marjorie Kinnan Rawlings: Part One," p. 18.

6. Kinnan Family archives, Phoenix, Arizona.

7. The poem is quoted in full, in an article about Mrs. Rawlings by Ernest L. Meyer, a good friend and fellow staff member of the University of Wisconsin literary magazine in 1917, in the June 10, 1938, issue of the *New York Post* (Kinnan Family archives, Phoenix, Arizona). Mr. Meyer here quotes from a letter to him by Mrs. Rawlings in which she says: " 'The type of writing that is natural to me— quick, splashy, overwritten—is bad writing. It has taken me all these years to learn to work under my own thumbscrews. If I let go the least bit, I can still turn out the most hopeless mess you'd wish to see.' "

8. Kinnan Family archives, Phoenix, Arizona.

9. This story, with its Hardyan ending, is included in Mrs. Rawlings' story collection, *When the Whippoorwill* (New York, 1943). The quotation is on p. 129.

10. "Keeping Posted," *The Saturday Evening Post,* April 26, 1947, p. 10; *ibid.,* May 31, 1947, p. 10.

11. Bigelow, *Frontier Eden,* p. 63.

12. The expansion of "A Mother in Mannville" into *Mountain Prelude* is described briefly in Bigelow's *Frontier Eden,* pp. 154–55. According to the slightly different account in the "Keeping Posted" section of *The Saturday Evening Post,* April 26, 1947, p. 10, there was a strong reader response to the original story, and people wanted to know what became of the little boy. Mrs. Rawlings, for her part, felt that the story was unfinished and so she wrote a longer version, showing how she would wish the tale to end. Metro-Goldwyn-Mayer bought *Mountain Prelude* almost before she sat down to write it. Understandably, in view of its very poor quality, it was not made into a movie nor was it published in book form.

13. Bigelow, *op cit.,* p. 155.

14. In *When the Whippoorwill,* p. 246.

15. "A Mother in Mannville" has had a curious attraction for readers over the years. It was included in the college anthology *Short Stories for English Courses,* edited by Rosa M. R. Mikels, revised by Helen T. Munn (New York, 1960), and at least four other anthologies, although Julia Bigham did not include it in her 1956 collection, *The Marjorie Rawlings Reader.* It was also reprinted in the April, 1965, issue of *Parents' Magazine & Better Homemaking,* and condensed and reprinted in the February, 1968, issue of *Reader's Digest.* For a

listing of Mrs. Rawlings' anthologized stories, see *Studies in Short Fiction*, Winter, 1970, p. 196.

16. *Mountain Prelude*: Part One, *The Saturday Evening Post*, April 26, 1947, p. 67.

17. *Mountain Prelude*: Part Two, *The Saturday Evening Post*, May 3, 1947, pp. 37, 137.

18. *Mountain Prelude*: Part Three, *The Saturday Evening Post*, May 10, 1947, pp. 146–47.

19. *Mountain Prelude*: Part Six, *The Saturday Evening Post*, May 31, 1947, p. 40.

20. *Ibid.*, p. 46.

21. "In the Heart," *Collier's*, February 3, 1940, p. 39.

22. "The Provider," *Woman's Home Companion*, June, 1941, p. 61.

23. "The Friendship," *The Saturday Evening Post*, January 1, 1949, pp. 14–15, 44.

24. Bigelow in *Frontier Eden*, pp. 153–54, discusses Mrs. Rawlings' neglect by the critics and describes the curve of her popular reputation (total obscurity to worldwide fame to semiobscurity), pointing out, however, that *The Yearling* has continued over the years to appeal strongly to young readers.

25. Bigelow, *op. cit.*, p. 19. A general summary of the Rawlings-Perkins correspondence on *The Yearling* is given on pp. 19–22.

26. Wheelock, ed., *Editor to Author*, p. 84.

27. Bigelow, *op. cit.*, p. 19.

28. Julia Bigham, "Introduction," *The Marjorie Rawlings Reader*, p. xv.

29. *Ibid.*, p. xvi.

30. Wheelock, *op. cit.*, p. 86.

31. Bigham, *op cit.*, p. xvi.

32. Bigelow, *op. cit.*, pp. 20–21.

33. Bigham, *op. cit.*, p. xvii.

34. Wheelock, *op. cit.*, p. 113.

35. Bigelow, *op. cit.*, p. 21.

36. Letter to me from M. A. Wright, Linville Falls, North Carolina, January 6, 1965.

37. Wheelock, *op. cit.*, pp. 135–36.

38. Paul Brooks, "Oklawaha," p. 36.

39. Bigelow, *op. cit.*, pp. 79–80.

40. Quoted in Harry Evans, "Marjorie Kinnan Rawlings: Part One," *The Family Circle*, May 7, 1943, p. 18.

41. Quoted in Bigelow, *op. cit.*, p. 138.

42. Mrs. Rawlings' profound hatred of cities, of which so much is made in her writings, seems on closer analysis almost an irrational phobia.

43. Edward T. Hall, *The Hidden Dimension*, Anchor Books Edition (Garden City, N.Y., 1969), p. 1.

44. Bigelow, *op. cit.*, pp. 92–93.

45. Donald W. Heiney, *Essentials of Contemporary Literature* (Great Neck, N.Y., 1954), p. 156. To simplify somewhat the publishing history of Steinbeck's novelette: the first three of the four parts of *The Red Pony* were published in a single volume in 1937, and all four parts were included in Steinbeck's *The Long Valley*, published in 1938. In Joseph Fontenrose's monograph *John Steinbeck: An Introduction and Interpretation* (New York, 1963), pp. 63–66, the reader will find interesting comments on "Jody Tiflin's passage from naïve childhood to the threshold of adulthood through knowledge of birth, old age, and death, gained through experience with horses." Fontenrose also draws a brief comparison of *The Red Pony* with Faulkner's *The Bear*—"in which the boy Ike McCaslin [reaches] manhood and understanding through experience in hunting and his relation to the great bear." The present writer wishes to thank a colleague, Dr. Ralph Bobb, for calling his attention to Steinbeck's "Jody" story in connection with *The Yearling*.

46. Bigelow, *op. cit.*, pp. 22, 154.

47. Amy Porter, "Growth of *The Yearling*," *Collier's*, September 29, 1945, p. 77.

48. *Ibid.*

Chapter Five

1. This saying is quoted in the first story in *When the Whippoorwill* ("A Crop of Beans") and elsewhere in Mrs. Rawlings' writings.

2. "Cocks Must Crow" would thus fit Mrs. Rawlings' vigorous, Webster-based definition of "regional literature," in which high standards of excellence are set for what constitutes literature. See her paper "Regional Literature of the South," *College English*, I (February, 1940), 381–88.

3. By the time she wrote *The Sojourner*, time may have ceased to pose such a threat. See for example *The Sojourner*, pp. 152–53, for a very different view of time held by the protagonist, whose thinking resembles that of Mrs. Rawlings in certain important ways.

4. Kenneth S. Lynn, ed., *The Comic Tradition in America*, Anchor Books Edition (Garden City, N.Y., 1959), p. 232. In his notes to Herman Melville's short story on this theme, "Cock-A-Doodle-Doo! or the Crowing of the Noble Cock Beneventano," Lynn discusses Melville's use of the crowing rooster and its use by a number of other writers of the period.

5. See Constance Rourke, *American Humor: A Study of the National Character*, Anchor Books Edition (Garden City, N.Y., 1955), chapter 2, "The Gamecock of the Wilderness," pp. 37–69.

6. *Ibid.*, pp. 39–40.

7. For a very different point of view elsewhere in Mrs. Rawlings' fiction, see the ending of chapter 26 of *The Yearling*. Here Grandma Hutto insists that certain troublemakers (the Forresters) *not* be brought to account for destroying her home. Her pacifist stand (taken to avert bloodshed) silences all protest, and the issue of vindicating one's manhood at the sound of a clarion call to action is not taken up.

8. Bigelow, *Frontier Eden*, p. 17. He refers to her as a "young woman," but in the story she looks "weathered gray" and is referred to as middle-aged.

9. *Ibid.*, p. 74.

10. *Ibid.*, p. 20.

11. *Ibid.*, pp. 132–33, 156.

12. *Ibid.*, p. 114.

Chapter Six

1. The resulting "Cross Creek Trial" is touched on in the first chapter of this book. A more extensive discussion of the trial is given on pp. 41–46 of Bigelow's *Frontier Eden*.

2. Bigelow, *Frontier Eden*, p. 76.

3. *Ibid.*, p. 124.

4. *Ibid.*, p. 143.

5. Larry E. Taylor, *Pastoral and Anti-Pastoral Patterns in John Updike's Fiction* (Carbondale, Ill., 1971), pp. 5–6.

6. *Ibid.*, p. 9.

7. *Ibid.*, p. 11.

8. Bigelow, *op. cit.*, pp. 120–21.

9. "I Sing While I Cook," *Vogue*, February 15, 1939, p. 48. Other culinary notes were published in various magazines in 1942.

10. Mrs. Rawlings' maternal grandmother, whose name was Traphagen, came from Michigan. An unusual lady, she is briefly described in a candid, affectionate memoir by Mrs. Rawlings, "Fanny—You Fool!," *Vogue*, July 15, 1942, p. 42.

Chapter Seven

1. Mrs. Rawlings' decline as a writer, which coincided with her virtual departure from Cross Creek, must be considered in the light of all that happened to her following her marriage in 1941 and the publication of *Cross Creek* in 1942. Bigelow, in *Frontier Eden*, pp. 38–52, details her tribulations and distractions during this unhappy period of decay.

2. Louis Bromfield in *The Saturday Review*, XXXVI (January 3, 1953), 9.

3. Edward Weeks in *The Atlantic Monthly*, CXCI (January, 1953), 80.

4. Riley Hughes in *Catholic World*, CLXXVI (March, 1953), 471.

5. Bigelow, *Frontier Eden*, p. 148.

6. *Ibid.*, pp. 47–48, 144–46.

7. Bigelow refers to "the Michigan area which was to be the setting for the new book" (p. 50, and cf. pp. 51, 144), but there is a natural confusion here. Mrs. Rawlings, who spent a considerable amount of the time devoted to producing *The Sojourner* in the upstate New York community of Van Hornesville, found in that region the same kind of farm land her grandfather had worked in Michigan (Bigelow, *Frontier Eden*, p. 50). But early in the novel the setting is clearly indicated: "inland from the Hudson River valley" (12).

8. See *The Sojourner* (12) and the news feature story on Mrs. Rawlings by Jane Quinn in the *St. Augustine* (Florida) *Record*, March 15, 1942. Substantiation of Mrs. Rawlings' ancestry as described above is to be found in the records of her paternal aunts (Misses Grace and Wilmer Kinnan of Phoenix, Arizona), who have compiled elaborate genealogies of her various family lines.

9. Quoted in an interview-article about Anthony Burgess: Anthony Lewis, " 'I Love England, But I Will No Longer Live There,' " *The New York Times Magazine*, November 3, 1968, p. 49. In this fascinating study of a prominent man of letters and his attitudes toward people, places, and things, Burgess is revealed as a *self-made* Existentialist individual par excellence. And he faults his fellow Englishmen for lacking this quality of existential activism: " 'One rarely gets that impression in England. It's happened in one's sleep, it's happened behind one's back. One wakes up and finds girls in miniskirts, one wakes up and finds we have a welfare state. Things are done for us, the people are not involved, there are no barricades. There's no consciousness of the meaning of government, the meaning of community. These things are happening behind our backs all the time.' " (*Loc. cit.*)

10. William Barrett, *Irrational Man: A Study in Existential Philosophy* (Garden City, N.Y., 1958), p. 56.

11. Rod W. Horton and Herbert W. Edwards, *Backgrounds of American Literary Thought*, 2d ed. (New York, 1967), pp. 503–04.

12. Cited in a letter to me from the Reverend Arthur MacGillivray, S.J., of Boston College, Chestnut Hill, Massachusetts, January 3, 1965.

13. Bigelow, *op. cit.*, pp. 62–63.

14. *Ibid.*, p. 95.

15. Seemingly an echo of Wordsworth's "A Slumber Did My Spirit Seal."

16. M. Esther Harding, *Journey into Self* (New York, 1956), pp. 4–5.

Chapter Eight

1. Bigelow, *Frontier Eden*, p. 11.
2. Bigham, "Introduction," *The Marjorie Rawlings Reader*; pp. ix–x.
3. Bigelow, *op. cit.*, p. 157.
4. "Having Left Cities Behind Me," *Scribner's Magazine*, XCVIII (October, 1935), 246.
5. Samuel Irving Bellman, "Marjorie Kinnan Rawlings: A Solitary Sojourner in the Florida Backwoods," *Kansas Quarterly*, II (Spring, 1970), 78–87.
6. "The Shell," in Bigham, ed., *The Marjorie Rawlings Reader*, pp. 373–74.
7. Bigelow, *op. cit.*, pp. 65–67.
8. *Ibid.*, p. 65.

Selected Bibliography

What Gordon Bigelow said in *Frontier Eden: The Literary Career of Marjorie Kinnan Rawlings* still holds true: "Published scholarly writing about Mrs. Rawlings is sparse." A large collection of Rawlings manuscripts, letters, and other valuable materials is to be found at the University of Florida at Gainesville Library. Much smaller in scope is the private collection of Rawlings materials located, at least until recently, at the home of Mrs. Rawlings' paternal aunts in Phoenix, Arizona. The following bibliography is selective: many pieces of juvenilia, book reviews, newspaper features by and about Mrs. Rawlings, private letter collections, etc., are omitted, primarily because they are inaccessible to most readers. There is a journalistic side to Mrs. Rawlings which may actually be as important as her essay-writing side. But, since it is unusually difficult to track down all or most of her newspaper contributions, she may never get the recognition for these that she probably deserves. In developing this bibliography I have made extensive use of the indispensable "Checklist of Publications" in *Frontier Eden*, pp. ii–iv (which, however, has a number of typographical errors).

PRIMARY SOURCES

1. Novels
   South Moon Under. New York: Charles Scribner's Sons, 1933.
   Golden Apples. New York: Charles Scribner's Sons, 1935.
   The Yearling. New York: Charles Scribner's Sons, 1938.
   The Sojourner. New York: Charles Scribner's Sons, 1953.

2. Other Volumes
   When the Whippoorwill. New York: Charles Scribner's Sons, 1943.
   Mrs. Rawlings' only story collection.
   Cross Creek. New York: Charles Scribner's Sons, 1942. Geograph-
   ical autobiography; reflects her experiences in and around
   her North Florida home since the late 1920s.
   Cross Creek Cookery. New York: Charles Scribner's Sons, 1942.
   Conversational cookbook; supplements *Cross Creek.*

The Secret River. New York: Charles Scribner's Sons, 1955. Post-humously published story for very young readers. Of interest only to students of Mrs. Rawlings' work.

3. Short Pieces

"The Reincarnation of Miss Hetty." *McCall's Magazine,* August, 1912, pp. 27, 72. Fiction.

"Cracker Chidlings: Real Tales From the Florida Interior." *Scribner's Magazine,* LXXXIX (February, 1931), 127–34. A string of fictionalized anecdotes.

"Jacob's Ladder," *Scribner's Magazine,* LXXXIX (April, 1931), 351–66, 446–64. Fiction. Included in *When the Whippoorwill.*

"Plumb Clare Conscience." *Scribner's Magazine,* XC (December, 1931), 622–26. Fiction. Included in *When the Whippoorwill.*

"A Crop of Beans." *Scribner's Magazine,* XCI (May, 1932), 283–90. Fiction. Included in *When the Whippoorwill.*

"Gal Young Un." *Harper's,* CLXV (June, 1932), 21–33; (July, 1932), 225–34. Fiction. Included in *When the Whippoorwill.*

"Hyacinth Drift." *Scribner's Magazine,* XCIV (September, 1933), 169–73. Nonfiction. Included in *Cross Creek.*

"Alligators." Written with Fred Tompkins. *The Saturday Evening Post,* CCVI (September 23, 1933), 16–17, 36, 38. Anecdotal fiction. Included in *When the Whippoorwill.*

"Benny and the Bird Dogs." *Scribner's Magazine,* XCIV (October, 1933), 193–200. Fiction. Reprinted in *Scholastic: The National High School Weekly,* March 2, 1935. Included in *When the Whippoorwill.*

"The Pardon." *Scribner's Magazine,* XCVI (August, 1934), 95–98. Fiction. Included in *When the Whippoorwill.*

"Having Left Cities Behind Me." *Scribner's Magazine,* XCVIII (October, 1935), 246. Poem.

"Varmints." *Scribner's Magazine,* C (December, 1936), 26–32, 84–85. Fiction. Included in *When the Whippoorwill.*

"A Mother in Mannville." *The Saturday Evening Post,* CCIX (December 12, 1936), 7, 33. Fiction. Reprinted in *Parents' Magazine & Better Homemaking* (April, 1965); condensed and reprinted in *Reader's Digest* (February, 1968). Included in *When the Whippoorwill.*

"Mountain Rain." *Scribner's Magazine,* CIV (July, 1938), 63. Poem.

"I Sing While I Cook." *Vogue,* XCIII (February 15, 1939), 48–49. Nonfiction. Culinary note.

"Cocks Must Crow." *The Saturday Evening Post,* CCXII (November 25, 1939), 5–7, 58, 60, 62–64. Fiction. Included in *When the Whippoorwill.*

"The Pelican's Shadow." *The New Yorker,* XV (January 6, 1940), 17–19. Fiction.

"The Enemy." *The Saturday Evening Post,* CCXII (January 20, 1940), 12–13, 32, 36, 39. Fiction. Included in *When the Whippoorwill.*

"In the Heart." *Collier's,* CV (February 3, 1940), 19, 39. Fiction. This material appears in somewhat altered form in chapter 16, "Black Shadows," of *Cross Creek.*

"Regional Literature of the South." *College English,* I (February, 1940), 381–88. Nonfiction. A very important editorial note is appended, pp. 388–89, containing personal details of Mrs. Rawlings' life and work based on informal remarks by the author. An important comment on *The Yearling* is given on p. 389: "For the depiction of the whole life of the boy the year's cycle was necessary, and the swift push into manhood required the sacrifice of the thing which he loved best."

"Jessamine Springs." *The New Yorker,* XVII (February 22, 1941), 19–20. Fiction.

"The Provider." *The Woman's Home Companion,* LXVIII (June, 1941), 21, 44, 46, 48, 60–61. Fiction.

"Here Is Home." *The Atlantic,* CLXIX (March, 1942), 277–85. Nonfiction. Included in *Cross Creek.*

"Who Owns Cross Creek?" *The Atlantic,* CLXIX (April, 1942), 439–50. Nonfiction. Included in *Cross Creek.*

"Fanny—You Fool!" *Vogue,* C (July 15, 1942), 42. Nonfiction. Memoir of Mrs. Rawlings' maternal grandmother.

"Sweet Talk, Honey!" *Vogue,* C (December 1, 1942), 77, 116–118. Nonfiction. Culinary note.

"Cross Creek Breakfasts." *The Woman's Home Companion,* LXIX (November, 1942), 72–73. Nonfiction. Culinary note.

"Trees for Tomorrow." *Collier's,* CXVII (May 8, 1943), 14–15, 24–25. Nonfiction. Note on conservation.

"Shell." *The New Yorker,* XX (December 9, 1944), 29–31. Fiction.

"Black Secret." *The New Yorker,* XXI (September 8, 1945), 20–23. Fiction.

"Miriam's Houses." *The New Yorker,* XXI (November 24, 1945), 29–31. Fiction.

Mountain Prelude. A six-part serial. *The Saturday Evening Post,* CCXIX (April 26, 1947), 15 et seq.; (May 3, 1947), 36 et seq.; (May 10, 1947), 38 et seq.; (May 17, 1947), 40 et seq.; (May 24, 1947), 36 et seq.; (May 31, 1947), 40 et seq.

Fiction. A novelette which includes and greatly expands "A Mother in Mannville."

"The Friendship." *The Saturday Evening Post*, CCXXI (January 1, 1949), 14–15, 44. Fiction.

4. Letters from Others

[Glasgow, Ellen] *Letters of Ellen Glasgow*. Edited by Blair Rouse. New York: Harcourt, Brace and Company, 1958. Contains two significant letters: one to Maxwell Perkins about *The Yearling*, and one to Mrs. Rawlings about *Cross Creek*. See pp. 247–48, 293–94.

[Perkins, Maxwell E.] *Editor to Author: The Letters of Maxwell E. Perkins*. Edited by John Hall Wheelock. New York: Charles Scribner's Sons, 1950. Included here are eleven letters from Mr. Perkins to Mrs. Rawlings, written between October 27, 1933, and June 10, 1946.

SECONDARY SOURCES

BELLMAN, SAMUEL I. "Marjorie Kinnan Rawlings," *The American Poet*, Winter, 1970, p. 33. Reprinted in *Golden Quill Anthology 1970*. Francestown, New Hampshire: The Golden Quill Press, 1970. P. 21. Poem.

———. "Marjorie Kinnan Rawlings: A Solitary Sojourner in the Florida Backwoods." *Kansas Quarterly*, II (Spring, 1970), 78–87. Introduction to Mrs. Rawlings' life and work.

BIGELOW, GORDON E., ed. "Marjorie Kinnan Rawlings' 'Lord Bill of the Suwannee River.'" *Southern Folklore Quarterly*, XXVII (1963), 113–31. Contains a five-page introduction. "Lord Bill" is a series of sketches that Mrs. Rawlings attempted, unsuccessfully, to publish as a story. See Bigelow, *Frontier Eden*, pp. 14, 132.

———. "Marjorie Kinnan Rawlings' Wilderness." *The Sewanee Review*, LXXIII (Spring, 1965), 299–310. Excellent introduction to Mrs. Rawlings' career as a writer; gives proper attention to her Florida backwoods environment.

———. *Frontier Eden: The Literary Career of Marjorie Kinnan Rawlings*. Gainesville, Fla.: University of Florida Press, 1966. Only literary biography of Mrs. Rawlings up to the present.

BIGHAM, JULIA SCRIBNER, ed. Introduction to *The Marjorie Rawlings Reader*. New York: Charles Scribner's Sons, 1956. Pp. ix–xix. Invaluable for its background on Mrs. Rawlings' relations with Scribner's and for its inclusion of some of the Rawlings-Perkins correspondence. The *Reader* contains the complete text of *South Moon Under* and selections from *Cross Creek*, *The Yearling*, and

When the Whippoorwill, as well as three other stories ("Jessamine Springs," "The Pelican's Shadow," and "The Shell").

BROOKS, PAUL. "Oklawaha: 'The Sweetest Water-Lane in the World.'" *Audubon*, LXXII (July, 1970), 34–36, 41–45. Included within the pages of this article is a color-photograph portfolio by Patricia Caulfield, "The Oklawaha Unspoiled," pp. 37–40. Important descriptive study of the geography and topography of northern Florida, which encompasses the "Rawlings country."

EVANS, HARRY. "Marjorie Kinnan Rawlings." In two parts. *The Family Circle*, May 7, 1943, pp. 10–11, 15, 17–18; May 14, 1943, pp. 20–21, 28, 30. Excellent introduction to the author.

POPE, VERNON. "Marjorie Rawlings Hunts for Her Supper." *The Saturday Evening Post*, CCXV (January 30, 1943), 26–27, 58–59. Pictorial local color.

PORTER, AMY. "Growth of *The Yearling*." *Collier's*, CXVI (September 29, 1945), 74–75, 77. Illustrated account of the filming of *The Yearling*.

Index

DATE DUE

GAYLORD			PRINTED IN U.S.A